The Italian Townscape

The Italian Townscape

by IVOR DE WOLFE

sketches and plans drawn by Kenneth Browne

photographs by IVY DE WOLFE

George Braziller, New York

To
CECCO and PRISCILLA

BASCHIERI SALVADORI

Published 1966 by George Braziller, Inc.,
by arrangement with The Architectural Press, London

Library of Congress Catalog Card Number: 66-10392

Printed in Great Britain

Contents

Acknowledgements

All the photographs in this book, some of which appeared in *The Architectural Review* of June 1962, are by Ivy de Wolfe with the following exceptions, for which the author expresses his gratitude: Aerofilms, figure 120. R.I.B.A., 128. Priscilla Baschieri Salvadori, 8, 206, 209, 239, 261. J. C. G. Hastings, 315. Technological Office of the Municipality of Rome, 409, 410, 411, 412, 413, 414, 415, 416, 417, 418, 419, 420, 421, 422, 423.

Many historical facts on the building of Sabbioneta have been uncovered by John Fleming and Reyner Banham, and information about floodlighting in Rome comes from Georgina Masson.

The author also wishes to express his thanks to Kenneth Browne for the sketches, pages 52 to 71, to Frederick Gibberd for permission to reproduce diagrams on page 209, and to his publisher Cluny Gillies of the Architectural Press for bringing order out of chaos.

Towns visited

1 Rome	88-89 Brescia	184 Padua
2 Florence	90-91 Florence	185-186 Florence
3-7 Venice	92-95 Orvieto	187 Limone
8 Baunei	96-97 Manciano	188 Iseo
9 Montefiascone	98-99 Viterbo	189 Florence
10 Capodimonte	100 Manciano	190 Iseo
11 Montefiascone	101-104 Viterbo	191 Porto Santo
12-13 Pitigliano	105-108 Perugia	Stefano
14 Posticciola	109 Bologna	192 Pitigliano
15 Florence	110 Padua	193 Lake Garda
16 Pitigliano	111 Bologna	194 Roccasinibalda
17 Florence	112 Norcia	195-196 Tarquinia
18 Marta	113-115 Bologna	197 Ravenna
19 Porto Santo	116 Assisi	198 Rome
Stefano	117 Sabbioneta	199 Venice
20 Lazise	118 Palmanova:	200 Rome
21-22 Urbino	1st plan	201 Pitigliano
23 Montefiascone	119 Sforzinda	202 Venice
24-25 Alassio	120 Palmanova: as	203-204 Viterbo
26-27 Perugia	built	205 Pitigliano
28 Spoleto	121-151 Sabbioneta	206 Baunei
29 Perugia	152 Rome	207 Venice
30-35 Urbino	153-156 Venice	208 Pitigliano
36-37 Ascoli Piceno	157-158 Rome	209 Manfredonia
38 Orvieto	159 Perugia	210-214 Sabbioneta
39 Bergamo	160 Verona	215 Bologna
40-41 Ascoli Piceno	161 Montefiascone	216-217 Urbino
42-47 Ascoli Piceno	162 Verona	218 Marta
48 Tarquinia	163 Iseo	219 Loreto
49-50 Florence	164-165 Florence	220 Florence
51-54 Perugia	166 Perugia	221 Lazise
55-56 Orvieto	167 Bergamo	222 Loreto
57-58 Lazise	168 Avezzano	223 Campobasso
59-61 Bergamo	169 Loreto	224-225 Padua
62-63 Fara Sabina	170 Florence	226 Rome
64-65 Florence	171 Loreto	227 Perugia
66-67 Foligno	172-173 Lazise	228 Ravenna
68-69 Padua	174 Rome	229 Vicenza
70-71 Orvieto	175 Bolsena	230 Lazise
72-73 Padua	176 Rome	231 Bolsena
74-75 Bergamo	177 Ravenna	232 Viterbo
76-77 Florence	178 Ascoli Piceno	233 Assisi
78-79 Bergamo	179 Rome	234 Rome
80-81 Orvieto	180 Orvieto	235-236 Assisi
82-83 Padua	181 Viterbo	237-238 San Marino
84-85 Orvieto	182 Siena	239 Baunei
86-87 Iseo	183 Verona	240-241 Imola

1

Townscape

When a hundred thousand breakfast tables are loaded every day 8 a.m., winter and summer, rain or fine, with bacon, planning may be said to be a fairly highly developed science. When they, the breakfast tables, are concentrated at twelve foot centres more or less, and the bacon is still brought home, *town*-planning, the art of getting bacon to breakfast tables when they are densely packed, is operating too.

The question then arises, is a congestion of breakfast tables a nice or nasty thing to have? One answer depends on whether congestion brings home the bacon better than uncongestion. Another on whether congestion is in its own right the greater pleasure. Which leads one to consider the larger meaning of these terms. Which involves their history. Which demonstrates a curious fact, namely that a large section of the human race *prefers* congestion to uncongestion and always has.

There have been a number of variables responsible for this preference— protection, water, money, liberty—and one constant, the hunch that society exists in its communications and congestion makes easier the contacts between man and man. A correct hunch—society *is* its contacts. *Is* its contacts in the sense in which the telephone system *is* its contacts. Three thousand million contacts the telephone system of this country owns to at the time of going to press, human society many more. Hence the citizen's brush with his bacon: the end term of a complicated series between man and man and man and pig—feeder and breeder, auctioneer, buyer, transporter, the chaps at the slaughter house, the chaps at the bacon factory, pre-packer, wholesaler, retailer, housewife, shopping basket, citizen, breakfast table. By the standards of modern organization a simple series of operations, in fact highly complicated, but, complicated or simple, a demonstration that the satisfaction of a desire as elementary as that for breakfast requires a long line of social contacts. When a strike of transport workers leaves the table empty the citizen may have harsh things to say about railwaymen or lorry drivers—evil communications corrupt good manners—but so long as the contact is re-established society does not suffer. A failure to reconnect, however, would reduce that society by precisely the extent of the failure. When contacts are loose we speak of country, when close and complicated, of town, when organized, of town-planning. Out of town-planning grows civic design, the study of the emerging pattern, out of civic design townscape, an art which by definition gives the bye (as Oliver Cromwell would say) to bacon and the various ways of bringing it home. Gives the bye, indeed, to nearly all else by abstracting from the dozens that matter one issue and one only—the question whether the artificial world created by congestion and called town has charms to offer. What those charms are. How to encompass them. Whether they provide the kind of frame people will cultivate congestion to get. If the end-product is going to be a lemon, all that work building and making roads and sewers would hardly seem worth while.

This is an argument which in any but the immediate past simply didn't arise. The debate was not as to whether *the city*, collective and abstract, was in itself desirable, but whether one desirable city rated higher than another —in desirability, that is—desirability being the sine qua non of a product universally accepted as the greatest artefact of man. Thomas Aquinas's *civitas communitas perfecta est* voiced a proposition self-evident to kings, for whom city-building was an investment in immortality, to philosophers, for whom the good life was by tradition allegorically described in terms of ideal town-planning, and to wizards, for whom a street lay-out offered a wonderful opportunity to make magic in 3-D. Thus Alexander. Thus Plato, the first Beaux Arts planner (and the worst). Thus Sir Thomas More. Thus Filarete and Campanella. Thus the Church, stealing a march on the others with a blue-print of two-cities-for-the-price-of-one, Jerusalem and Babylon, the first unutterably good, the second inconceivably evil. Evil, not dull. No one ever suggested Babylon was dreary. That was the trouble. It was so hideously inviting, wickedness and all.

Came the storm. Blake's dark satanic mills (which he never saw) elbowed out Jerusalem while naughty no longer, simply dull—dirty and dull— Babylon vanished in the smoke. City became a dirty word, and thing; the citizens determined to opt out, and did, leap-frogging over each other's homes by rail or road till brought up all standing by the sea. The flight from the town: with England, the first and still the worst victim of the industrial revolution, leading both the retreat and the attack on the urban thing.

The retreat continues today, so does the attack, the one encouraged by the automobile, the other, oddly enough, by the town-planners, British and American. Prior to the birth of Cumbernauld and miscarriage of Hook to raise one's voice in the cause of congestion was equivalent to admitting a fetish for tight-lacing. You weren't nice to know and the planners let you know it, being, all but a small handful, addicts of the Aertex shirt and string vest. Three Aertex types prevail today headed by the fuddy-duddies for whom an Englishman's home is his garden. Hence the garden-city, the leap-frogger's dream, valid as a protest against slum and smog, but in its present, last, degenerate phase a mere open invitation to prairie planning and to that extent a menace to the social body as the private garden is to family unity.*

Then there are the collaterals of the modernist junior branch, the light-and-air men, who apply under the rheumy eye of their leader (le Corbusier) landscape gardening principles in the only place where they are unsuitable, the urban thing. Airy as against prairie planning. Enormous point blocks separated from the world and each other by tracts of landscaped park. There is as it happens one place in the town where landscape principles could apply—the street—but here, ironically enough, the Airies in their eyries capitulate to the traffic engineer.

Finally there are the radicals for whom old-hat stuff about Togetherness is mere reactionary twaddle. Present objective, custom-built anti-towns with drive-in shops sited out there on the veldt for the greater convenience of a car-using race. The ex-urban ideal. Result, the gaseous society, spread like Antares thinly through space for four hundred million miles or so (if lineal add another nought). It is the practical consequences of his ideas the radical hates to tangle with. He lives not in a praire nor in an airy but in a fairy world full of unfurling wings, prismatic colours, novel shapes, lost inhibitions, broken chains, radiant perspectives.

In fact, of course, all these approaches contain elements of worth—and of use—God preserve our radicals even when exhibiting the defects of their virtues—they only become dangerous when they are employed to obscure the one basic truth without which not only towns and town-planning but society itself loses all pretence of orientation. This can be stated in its most universal term by saying that society is everywhere at all times subject to the law of gravity. The gregarious law, that is to say, is the exact equivalent

* Dad wants flowers or vegetables, mum wants to hang out the washing, the kids are murder to both. Only solution, to murder the kids.

of the gravitational under which the attractive force of bodies varies directly as their mass and inversely as the square of the distance between them. Bodies of people included. Bodies of people *gravitate*. And gravitation, remember, doesn't pick and choose, but operates all round, dragging its victims back to the centre from every point of the compass. You may beat gravity—the second clause shows how swiftly the pull loses its grip—but so long as you remain within the gravitational field your natural movement is centripetal. Released from this field, social bodies which were once in orbit (suburbs) can fly off and drift away into space though sooner or later gravity will catch up with them, creating a new nucleus for development. Unless one accepts society as an organism obeying a gravitational law involving nucleated development the word society itself ceases to have a meaning.

There follows the only principle townscape is bound to acknowledge. We know it and we ignore it. The centre is a magnet. From that one law every other flows, including the law of density, which adds categorically that the only true happiness lies at the centre. This law, every gregarious person acknowledges generally in its converse—the further I have to walk to the shops, pubs, cinema, church, school, high-street—the further I have to push the pram—the less happy am I.

Townscape can thus be treated as the art of humanizing high densities after the engineers have made them hygienically possible. Dangerous that word after, but the fact has to be faced; one man's irresistible impulse to inflict himself on the next raises terrible problems for those of his buddies who have to work out the arrangements. So let's stick to *after*. *After* drains and hygiene have been taken care of the question arises how close you can live to your neighbour and like it. A few living close makes a town, a lot living close a city. Were our cities wicked but still desirable the question wouldn't arise, but the whole issue is prejudiced as we have seen by the disasters that have overtaken them. So much so that it has become normal to think of the city as a kind of purgatory in which one suffers the agony of the not-quite-damned in the cause of earning a living; and so long as this view persists it will be natural to think of it as a place to get out of. Or reform, reform being associated in the public mind with rebuilding in the grand manner, avenues, axes, triumphal arches, *rond-points* and the rest, as effective a substitute for real planning (involving real townscape) as are prepacked deep-frozen golden fish fingers for real food.

But this view must not persist. Babylon may be a bit too far to go back, but there is ample evidence nearer home to show that our predecessors, though weak on hygiene, made a major success of the art of living together, a success so major that a whole major industry, tourism, has developed out of the urge of the failures to go visiting the non-failures. So great is this traffic and so enormous its profits that the non-failures are now in danger of being trodden into the ground in their attempt to give hospitality (quotes) to the plug-uglies. Emblem of this conflict, the chara. To appreciate the predicament to the full go to Venice in the full moon and watch a guitarist serenading a chara-load of old ladies from a Lancashire cotton town, in a fleet of gondolas hired by a London travel agency as part of an all-in fourteen days' trip through fifteen countries and sixteen capitals. For none of the cotton-spinners is this a genuine experience (if it were it might be worth the price paid), it is merely an expensive investment in cyclorama at the cost of the loss of many cuppas. By no conceivable argument can the trip be said to have broadened their minds or fired their imaginations unless renaming number 23 Worsely Road, Capodimonte is to be so described. The most it and the suitcase labels that go with it will do is to serve, once back home, as yet another status symbol. As for the gondoliers and troubadours, the indignity is one only their sense of humour provides protection against. Cornered they would repeat the classic crack of Liberace when accused of a similar accommodation with Mammon, I cried all the way to the bank—witty, but in the last resort tragic. For Venice the whole thing is straight prostitution of the lowest canal-corner kind.

Let us be clear. No one wants to kill tourism. The need is to prevent it killing itself by destroying that which gives it its impetus. The need is to reverse the process by which the world becomes day by day more enslaved to boring uninteresting subtopia and less enslaved to wicked, exciting, dangerous, inviting Babylons. The need is to reverse the process because boring uninteresting subtopia breeds boring, uninteresting people who react on Babylon itself by making it boring and uninteresting. Destroying it in the name of progress. If that is progress the time has come to do something about it. And one of the things one can do is to make a study of the towns and cities people did once enjoy living in in order to rediscover the pleasures of urban life. Have they any message for modern town-planners?

The answer is yes, of many kinds, cautionary included. We propose to consider them in the following pages in a way some fundamentalists regard as superficial because it involves the eye, a view which seems to ignore the part played by that organ in the decisions of the reason—of more than the reason, the imagination, which, before it can get to work at all, has to be made pliable by visual exercise, briefed by memory, fed on what other imaginations have pumped up out of the sludge. The object of the exercise, to compile a case-book of the past in the interest of the present. Surprisingly novel the idea seems too, which shows the distance we have come since the days of pattern-book architecture, indeed, since the early days of architectural journalism—for the technique is the same. With this difference, that now that no one is going out to crib Portofino or Venetian Gothic, it is possible to listen-in to the past in a new way. Hence, as suggested above, this survey with its deliberate return to methods reminiscent of the lantern lecture in the church hall, choice of subject quite arbitrary, depending on which tour the vicar chose for his summer holiday—Italy, in this case, or rather half Italy, the part of the body above the belt, Italy being still two countries divided by history and the power of the sun.

But no, on second thoughts not quite so arbitrary as the vicar's lantern lecture. For the obligation here is to look for a period and place where townscape, if not a certified and licensed art, has been practised on the impulse by men who built what they loved and loved what they built. Could one in that case expect to fare better than in the sector of Europe where, by a strange miscalculation of destiny and business men and despite all that the Lambrettas can do to destroy them, many splendid towns have survived almost intact? Even now, little though she deserves it, Europe still possesses a great heritage of townscape, most of which has significance for the modern planner.

There is another reason for taking Italy as a model and that is the hope that it may remind Italians themselves of the need to protect this inheritance from the outrage that has happened elsewhere in the name of progress. The standard of living is racing up in the Italian peninsula; no one, least of all the townscaper, wants to see it stop. It throws the door open, however, to commercial exploitation posing as free enterprise, posing as progress posing as the thing that excuses any enormity in the developers' handbook of crime. Yet the solution is simple enough, to make it clear that outrage-in-the-name-of-progress is no longer acceptable. Now that science has provided enterprise with the power to consume its own excreta 'development' can at last be achieved without the mess traditionally accompanying it.

Italy is a young nation, far younger than the US, hardly a century old, a young nation with an old history, some of it grim. Yet less than twenty years after disaster in war her genius has reasserted itself in ways that make one wonder whether after all she will not always remain the centre of the civilized West. The secret is a special humorous earthy glamour, a property the new Romans have superimposed upon the post-war rat-race,

14

snatching in passing the bay-leaves from the brows of less supersonic sprinters—style and fashions from the French, movies and women from the Americans, from the British, gent's tailoring and sport. Both the glamour and the earthiness are reflected in the Italian way of life which is —hence its terrible fascination—at once more elementary and more virtuoso than those of its fellow democracies either side of the Atlantic.

And here lies the opportunity—and the danger. Wealth is stealing back into the chests of the Roman Empire and with it the power to defend its own entail or complete the crack-up of the estate.

The Three Faces of Italy

Plain speaking first. Italy has three faces, two of
which need to be tactfully demolished before we
can catch up with the one we want. Face A is the
brand-image or Façade Touristique which, like
the moon, presents always the same striking but
stagey mask to the world—sumptuous
photography of celebrated subjects, S. Peter's,
S. Mark's, the Capitol, 1, the Piazza Signoria at
Florence, 2. Grand but long ago milked dry of

1

2

Venice

3

meaning, and also a bit of a fraud in the sense that they are largely used by photographers as fig-leaves to conceal less savoury matters (page 189) lying beneath. The second face is cautionary. In certain sectors already a dread reality, and everywhere a potential threat but not yet engulfing (as it does in England) the whole civilization, industrial blight throws its shadow over the scene, dark already in the least expected places. The approaches to Venice for instance, 4, 5, 6, 7, some of which suggest the dead-cat-filled sewers of the Black Country, 3, rather than the Adriatic's pride. An honest picture of the Italian scene could hardly be drawn without some reference to these two false façades, one a mask, the other an eruption. That done we turn with

gratitude in all the pages that follow to the third, the natural smiling face, innocent of make-up and not as yet the victim of developer's rash if occasionally visited by a slight attack of acne or impetigo. These expressive features portray the real Italy whose genius has done so much to lighten our darkness by demonstrating (amongst other things) the deeper felicities of *towniness*, a property which involves no rejection of economic progress or modern building and engineering. It merely encourages the developers to see the world of the past as a living inheritance rather than a hang-over. And invites them, too, to use the new techniques and machines—excavator, bulldozer, hydraulic shovel—as instruments of evolution rather than weapons of destruction.

2

The New Art

Townscape is an art which demands no expertise, no training, no professionalism, no effort, no discipline, no mental feats. Not even strength of character. Apprenticeship to any profession normally requires years of dogged dedication. Here for once is a mystery to which one can dedicate oneself at a moment's notice— and become by the same token an expert, partly because there are no other experts, and partly because no greater skill is required of the adept than an ability to let events OUT THERE bounce off the retina of the eye, which they do anyway. His own contribution lies in admitting that the visual message doesn't always get through, for most of us are blind to the more entertaining aspects of the world, another way of saying we lose at an early age our visual curiosity.

Not without good reason. So vast are the responsibilities it is saddled with in getting a human soul safely through the crises and dangers of daily life that the eye quickly forms habits of selection under which the non-essential visual issues are shelved in favour of the vital ones (delicatessen-with-spit-chicken,

4
5
6
7

21

car-doing-eighty, good-legs). From one *point of view* valuable, from another a contraction of our legitimate interests in OUT THERE, one of which consists in the making of judgements as to how we want OUT THERE to look—how, that is, to create our own OUT THERE, build our own world. The greatest of all human activities, the building of a private, specifically humane environment ('town') against all the preconceptions of 'Nature'. Not to mention the gods. If *town* is that environment, *townscape* is the art of re-alerting the eye to its possibilities. Hardly a new art, since it has been practised for upwards of five thousand years (Babylon, you will remember, was a highly seductive place). Yet so long have all but the most elementary of its routines been in abeyance that most of the themes pursued here can reasonably be regarded as, if not novel, at any rate widely neglected, a situation we propose to exploit by treating this book as a primer.

An insultingly elementary one some may think, reading pages 47 and 48. For the moment, however, certain broader issues require investigation and under the title PROFILE get it. The word is meant to cover the build-up of whole towns or sections of towns as well as profiling in the stricter sense shown opposite, 8, where the buildings of Baunei are thrust up into the Sardinian sky in forms sufficiently unlikely to surprise and stimulate even the un-realerted eye.

Profiles

Profiles

Washing

First profile, washing. Idling in the sun or
blowing in the wind, this is often the first thing you
see approaching a town, beautiful gleaming human
washing. A reminder that we are all brothers and
sisters (and fathers and mothers) with a similar

11

need of soap. A reminder, too, that townscape is *not* town-planning, is *not* architecture, *is* the urban scene stock-piled with all its impedimenta, toys, trinkets, tools, services, conveniences, shelters, play-pens, people. Its topic, the public life of private lives, never better expressed than by beautiful gleaming washing publicly blowing or idling. Let us cherish it while we may; the rake's progress of the launderette suggests that it will soon be a period piece, bracketed with other obsolete Hogarthian practices, like pouring the slops into the street from top-floor windows.

Personality

It is—with few exceptions—difficult to identify an English town by its shape. Italian towns always seem to be able to pull a profile out of the hat. One of these is to be seen hiding behind the beautiful gleaming washing, Capodimonte, a conventionally beautiful shape. The striking thing, however, about Italian profiles is their variety. Like a friend, one is able to associate almost any given town with its physical outline. Nor is this merely because many can boast perimeters in the shape of town walls or hilltops.

The modelling ranges from the astonishing at Baunei, 8, and the sophisticated at Montefiasconi, 9, 11, to the elemental at Pitigliano, 12, 13, all small towns, the last two with titanic walls and medieval cleavage between town and wild (16 is a shot of Pitigliano's 'country' taken hanging over the town wall). Yet Posticciola, 14, with neither wall nor hilltop, rides the contours in just as memorable a way, one signature clearly stamped throughout from outskirt fringe effects to the articulations at the centre, culminating in the church tower. All, arguably, small towns, and so apt for profiling,

13

14, 15

but the river-front at Florence, 15, demonstrates that an articulation as precise can be achieved on the scale of a city. No trick of the camera, this, as the view from the Uffizi, 17, shows. Rather wonderful that a large industrial city which has been in the front line of war can keep its figure like that. Retain such character. Unique Florence is not but she is uniquely adept at putting across her *persona*. An evil one—desperately wicked.

Wickedness

Contemporary Florentines may not feel more diabolical than other men but in the collective bank they have a handsome capital of crime— starting with the first Tarquin and rolling on through Savonarola's burning, the diabolical sophistries of Machiavelli, the usurious commercial humanism (very wicked) of the Medicis,

16

elongates every form starting with the instrument of torture which is the tower of the Palazzo Vecchio and running through Etruscan enormities and evilly extruded roofs, 17. Even the colour crawls with vice. Most vicious of all, Vasari's Piazza to the Uffizi (itself an evil building if ever there was one) a shape so sinister that for once it is a relief to see those emblems of the banal, charas, 293, parked in this unnatural place. The river, too, has a cruel narrow straightness, like the scar of a razor slash or a murderer's mouth.

Character

The object of the above note is not, as might be thought, to establish Florence as a hot-spot of vice but to celebrate the triumph of a strong personality, for strong it must surely be to arouse such reactions. Ditto the Florentines, to have so doggedly preserved their wicked townscape. At the opposite end of the moral spectrum and in its own way just as individual stands the architecture of Simple Faith, Porto Santostefano for example, 19, home of fisherman and peasant, a model of unaffected composition. Not wicked—simple and salty, yet the build-up upon the cliff is worthy of Cannes. Marta's approaches, 18, are not so romantic but more oddly come by. The façade behind Api, so suggestive of Assembly Rooms in country towns, is in fact a screen which masks the Old Town from the advancing visitor and by this means fools him into turning left (to the main road) or right (to Lake Bolsena). If instead he insists on not being deflected, a startling metamorphosis occurs through the archway—Old

18

and the last Murder In The Cathedral (Giuliano's: much worse than Becket's—at Mass, at the moment of the Elevation of the Host, the preconcerted signal). However, moral turpitude doesn't have to be proved here—sufficient if the shapes of the buildings express it, and they do. Wickedness made stone. A congenital Mannerism

19

Town in every meaning of the word, complete with
old-world townees who do not take kindly to
photographs or photographers. Lucky if you escape
with your shirt. Somebody in the 16th century
must have decided the old town wasn't nice to know
and walled it in. He was right, and so are they.
20 isn't a novel shot of Ashridge Park but one of
Lazise's landward approaches. Difficult to believe
that the other side of the Town Wall set in this
sylvan scene is a thriving resort filled to the last
bidet with Germans in shorts and water-skiers in
less. Also a café-packed quay, harbour, lido,
caravan park, plage.

Street Profile

Streets are dealt with later. Here just a word on
the subject of street profile, bold generally,
sometimes better than bold, and often, when the
sky is brought into the game, matriculating from
profile to silhouette. Vernacular or monumental
doesn't matter, the nearly overlapping roofs in 21
are as good in their own way as the imposing series
of unlikely events which compose the Corso
Garibaldi at Urbino, 22. The gateway, 23, draws
attention to something common to all these
examples (not forgetting 8): their masterly way of
using—by trapping—the sky. Trapped sky. When
achieved, a feather in the designer's cap,
because—the art of town-making being the pursuit
of enclosure—he is under constant threat from
above. The big leak. Too much empty space up
there, threatening to come in and break the

whole thing up. Always remembering that in the
designer's vocabulary light and sky have different
meanings. In the past sky-trapping was a difficult
business in dull Northern climes. To-day
architectural techniques and taller buildings make
it something of a Must.

23

24

34

Vernaculars

Every street can't, of course, have Urbino's Palazzo
Ducale to give it drama, but character manifests
in many forms. What could be more brilliant
than the front at Alassio with its tall foreground,
low middle-distance, and final arrow-head kick-up.
Here, 24, one can see how lucky or clever the
Italians have been in having no Victoriana to
clutter things up. Their architecture steps
straight out of the eighteenth into the twentieth
century, in the company of two vernaculars, one
peasant, the other middle class, neither of which
need flinch when elbowed by a modern building.
The Mediterranean and Riviera styles. The two
houses on the left, 25, belong to the past in time
and to the beautiful gleaming washing (of which
there is an abundance here) in social standing, but
they have no quarrel of any visual sort with the
tall new bourgeois next door. Hence the wonderful
homogeneity of Italian towns, even the big ones
like Perugia, a capital city, 26, 29. Many of the
buildings in the general view are modern but there
are no sore thumbs.

26

27

28

Segregation

It is the sanity of the ploy, here at Perugia, which is so impressive. The City, 26, is built on more hills than one, each so steep the knees of the pedestrian wobble on sight, or would had this almost magic cat-walk, 29, not materialized to waft them (the knees) from one mountain to the other. The arc of its course can be clearly followed through the distant buildings on the route to round and Romanesque S. Angelo. Sane because romantic, charming and cheap. For once the pedestrian is not penalized, it is the traffic (as is only right and proper since it carries the HP) that has to take the dive or do the other thing, in this case, go under, 27. The photograph prompts thoughts of another cultural capital with a similar traffic problem and population (both are slightly under 100,000), Oxford. Rather pathetic, the Christchurch meadow quarrel, now, actively pursued for rising half a century, when you consider that hard-up Perugia can afford to build a tunnel under the whole town and rich Oxford can't even bring itself to dig a little ditch. Another way of segregating traffic and pedestrians is practised at one-hill Spoleto, 28, pedestrians going straight up and the traffic being made to go round and around. Sanity again. It's a steep pull if you're walking but you make the top so soon after the roadster that the action takes on the air of a conjuring trick.

Town and Country

'Town' and 'Country' in Italy are still realities.
They are also as often as not neighbours, a fact
which, as we have seen, multiplies the
opportunities for profiling. The distinction at
Urbino, 31, is wonderfully maintained but can it
go on? Obviously when expansion occurs building
development could only be kept inside the walls
at the cost of pulling down the old town. Here
Italian policy is clear-cut and very sound: to do no
such thing. Instead, to build a bye-pass and use it
as the centre-of-gravity of new building.
Disadvantage, extra-mural development.

Profiles

Advantage, leaving the old town intact. One can't pretend there is no sprawl but it is canalised. And limited. The scene in 30 (a shot taken from the town wall) is not ideal, but subtopia in the form of the suffocating villadom that strangles every English town still hardly exists at all.

32

Precipitation

One good reason for being stingy with sky is the tendency of its users to ignore space. Like gravity, space operates everywhere and remains in consequence at a discount until manipulated in such a way as to re-attract the attention of the eye. Urbino is one more precipitous town with simple motto for motor coaches—Keep Out. How right too, but where are the buses and charas to go? The answer involves elevating a car park— in two meanings of the word. Physically, by raising it on a great brick arcade, 33, up to the plimsoll line of the town, 32. Psychologically, by

33

Profiles

34

turning the grimmest of all modern conveniences
into a first-rate piece of theatre by means of a
classic space-trick, the ha-ha. An invisible dyke
between the ground you stand on and the world
beyond, the ha-ha can be used civically as a
hazard for isolating one side from another, often
a useful traffic gambit. On the monumental scale
employed here it becomes a chasm (unseen but
deeply felt) between the huge platform hoisted
upon its brick arcade and the prospect beyond.
Result, the sudden precipitation of town and

country into each other's arms, 34, 35. Notice how
significantly the action is underlined by the thin
fine line of the platform's retaining wall. The
presence of that horizontal, with the foreknowledge
it gives of the huge drop beyond, prompts the eye
and the body after it to jump-and-be-damned,
whence arises in the mind of the beholder the urgent
preoccupation with space and space-travel advocated
above. Though nothing could be simpler, it would
be hard to find a more effective piece of urban
drama. The great red elephant of the palace, 34, and

35

white mouse of the Via Mazzini, 35, frame the
prodigious view, one foiling the other in a way
that makes clear at once the Italian contempt for
inflexible drawing-board mechanics or orthodox
attitudes to the monumental. Sitte had a word
for the Beaux Arts hang-over and all that went with
it in the shape of straight lines, right-angles,
symmetry, balance, rigid standardization of
pattern, inflexible geometrical routines—*artless*—
and so at one stroke cut the Grand Manner
planners down to size as naïve persons practising
banal and obvious tricks to the disgust of more
artful performers.

36

37

Narcissism

One of the advantages of hills lies in the
opportunity they provide for narcissism. A
promenade sited on the right contour line of a
spur will give all one needs in the way of flashback,
the town *from* the town, often the old town from
the new. A grave test of character. At Ascoli
Piceno, 36, the old town comes off fairly well, but
when one turns to the detail of the promenade, 37,
the full extent of the catastrophe is revealed:
suburban disaster. At one moment Italia in all
its simple strength, the next, a transformation of
the scene, brought about by a seat, a vulgar
lamp-post, a dwarf wall, ornamental treelets and
inappropriate planting.

3

The Street

The business so far has involved bulk deals only. Important as these are, the mainstream of townscape practice lies naturally enough in the street: net- rather than gross-work. Let us look at the prospect with the eyes of the tourist whirled into a strange town and instantly surrounded by a ring of hungry man-eating objects occupying a jungle of alleys through—or out of—which he has to fight his way. How is he to survive?

The answer is, divide and rule. Divide into *background*—the pattern of Civilia—and *objects*, the furniture of the place. Thus good townscape often comes out of bad architecture. Conversely good architecture often makes bad townscape. For the good reason that its real allegiance is not to architecture but to the stage where theatrical not architectural criteria apply. Hence its contempt for the kind of town-planning described by Camillo Sitte in his book, *The Art of Building Cities*, as the 'modern system of blocks and regularly aligned houses' with their 'inflexible geometrical principles'. The Beaux Arts ideal, whose 'straight lines and rectangles' he compares with the 'free inventiveness of the old masters'. He adds with emphasis 'we absolutely insist that the straight line and geometrical patterns should not be made the aims of our planning'.

That was in 1896. How little we have learnt in the years between can be judged by the kind of picture most of us conjure up when

43

we use the word *street*—two lines of parallel uniform buildings fencing a long straight artery through which the 'life-blood' of the city 'circulates', life-blood being conceived always in terms of vehicular traffic. Before modern times there was at least one period in Italy when, in revolt against the T-trap and egged on by restless prelates like Sixtus V, the vogue developed for long, narrow, too-straight-to-be-true streets lined with palazzos and ending with deplorable bathos in nothing. But recovery from this disease was speedy, which is a way of saying that the routines of the middle ages with their nests of alleys and nexus of buildings stayed on top. Amongst Northern cities only a few like the City of London itself (hence the traffic problem) still perpetuate the pattern (horribly mutilated); but in the South such exceptions are still the rule and except in the case of ancient Roman roads like the Cassia, which cleave a ruthless way through towns as well as country, the modern traffic artery tends to be parallel to rather than superimposed upon the old pattern whose principle was the exact converse of the one current to-day.

It was, that is to say, not a matter of laying out a street and aligning buildings along it, but of arranging a building group according to its requirements and then leaving an alley on the outside between one group and another. An academic distinction so long as modern corruptions obscure the street's essential nature as a precinct, a playground, a home-from-home, an escape —almost a retreat—from the various disciplines grinding service out of their victims in the bowels of the adjacent buildings. And true to its ideal as playground as well as service area the street spawned caves, inns, stalls, shops, the appurtenances of leisure, and in the process took on the aspects of a fair with the appropriate accompaniment of visual hazards in aid of cosiness, gaiety and convenience.

These refinements stupid officials in the higher latitudes of Europe have standardised out of existence by reducing the unit of the town to one hideous norm, the bye-law street, tarmac'd and office-or-villa-lined. In Italy, where that standardization has never been imposed, one gets a different picture of Civilia's possibilities.

The Street

38 39
40 41

45

42

Interior Street

At this point a difficult decision has to be faced—
whether to incur the reader's contempt by
embarking on a beginner's exercise in the A B C of
the art on the assumption that he is a novice,
or his fury by assuming a common ground that
doesn't exist. As one can't play safe, the reasonable

course seems to be to assume ignorance in the
novice and tolerance in the expert, who will probably
need it for the note which follows. It starts with
the eye's private conspiracy to defeat the purposes
of townscape by preferring people to their
background. Stage-blindness it might be called,
meaning aliveness to the actors, blindness to the

The Street

props. Those on page 45 for instance. By any
change in his reactions to these street scenes
before and after reading what follows the reader
can assess his own susceptibility to the disease.
If he has it bad, a good place to start will be a
church, preferably one big enough to have
something in common with the world *out there*
and high enough to allow the aisles to act as
interior streets, which in fact they are. The point
is that such streets are enclosed and so impose
visual limitations the real ones lack. Moreover,
inside a building a viewer is psychologically
predisposed to respond to visual stimuli. Something
else he is ready to accept as well: *intention*.
Whereas, outside, all but the crudest essays in
axiality and monumentality (Arc de Triomphe,
Place de la Concorde—planning, that)
will be ignored as accidental, inside, it stands
to reason someone must have contrived even the
side-effects, hence one can readily admit the
existence of an unseen mind exercising deliberate
intention. Accident or its appearance plays, as
it happens, an important part in the urban drama,
but so does intention disguised as such, and it is a
good working principle for the beginner to treat
any successful stage-effect, however accidental-
looking, as someone's brain-child. It probably was.
With that introduction let us enter one of the
world's least known but most beautiful churches,
S. Agostino, Ascoli Piceno, and see what it has
to offer in the way of townscape. First class
'theatre', right at the start in the shape of the
organ loft over the High Altar, 42. The one crucial
aesthetic mistake made by mediaeval architects
was in developing what is known to-day in
capitals as The East Window. Even with the
protective armour of stained glass no window in
that position can avoid blinding those who look
towards the altar, thus at one and the same time
defeating the purposes of ritual and the claims
of tourism. No such mistake was made here.
Rebuilt in 1490 the East End collected in course of
time, 42, a Baroque exercise in *trompe l'oeil* so
masterly that one has the greatest difficulty (on
the site as well as in the photograph) telling
whether the organ loft is real or imagined, or
whether there is a real or imagined organ in the
real or imagined organ loft. Anyway, what you see
in this picture is paint and nothing else, lit, one

43
44
45
46

47   48

would be ready to swear, either by stage floods
or a crafty photographer's flashlight, in fact by
the unaided day from a hidden window on the
North side of the chancel. No one in his senses
could suppose this superb piece of daylighting
to be anything but deliberately planned—to
achieve verisimilitude a deceit of this kind has
to be lighted from the source indicated by the
shadows in the painting—or that the various
stage effects, 43-46, by which the columns
of nave and aisle play cat and mouse with each
other and it, are unintended. Now turn,
remembering all this intention, to the South aisle,
47, and look up the serried perspective of
attached columns on the right which belong
in fact to no less than four altars in separate
bays of the church, coalescing into this
impressive composition only when so approached.
Was the effect intentional? Yes, and
very successful. And illustrates something even
more significant, the split instant in which
architecture becomes townscape. In linking one
altar visually with another whoever did it designed
a street, and that is exactly how the townscaper
has to see his raw materials, not as separate
altars in elevation but as related objects in
perspective. Get this business in perspective,
say the professors. Precisely. Every
situation has to be got into perspective, that is
into relation one object with another vis-a-vis
oneself. So sold were Baroque architects on
this view of their art that they started building
for perspective, thus producing, in designs like the
church at Tarquinia, 48, results not
dissimilar from the linked altars of Ascoli. Nor
were they the only ones. Turning back to
page 45, one can see now that the Palazzo
Nuovo at Bergamo, 39, was obviously designed with
an eye to its foreshortened effect. As for Ascoli's
Duomo, the head-on shot, 40, suggests
an eye preoccupied *mainly* with, 41, the

foreshortened effect. Not very logical in view
of its position, nevertheless, streets being what
they are, the foreshortened view is *normally* the
only view. And, buildings being on streets, the
view of them is normally the foreshortened view.
All of which adds up to what has just been said,
namely that a building is not its facade, seen in
elevation, but is the twisted, warped,
foreshortened object you normally see falsified
by perspective. Ditto for all the other objects
on the street. One warp is architecture, two are
townscape.*

* 'One building is architecture, two are townscape.' Gordon Cullen.

The Street

The Bias

These two pictures sum up what has just been said and offer both a statement of intention and declaration of interest. No concern here with the citizen going about his business, nor with all those tourists pouring through the Palazzo Vecchio, tidal-waving up the grand staircase of the Uffizi, cha-cha-cha-ing past Venus on her dizzy shell. Our business is with the street not with the picture-

gallery, the wall not the painting, the piazza not
the sculpture. Ignoring all that dishy stuff in the
Loggia dei Lanzi we gaze instead with passion at
the vista through its arcade, 49. Nearly impossible
to do under normal circumstances with so much
trivia about, including the girl at the no entry
sign, so let us switch the lighting so as to leave girl,
David, Cellini, Venus, the tourists, in the dark,
with all their rolleiflexes. The moment we do, the

spot-light swings from furniture to street, from
stage to stage-scenery, from foreground to background, and the town begins to do for the townscaper what it should have done from the start,
steal the show. And a wicked city Florence still
looks, with that diagonal stage-set drawing
one inexorably through the theatrical proscenium
arch to some desperate crime, political or passional,
in the shadows beyond.

51

Convex

52

convex

Let us now go out into the street and start walking. Though exploration of space is legitimate business for road engineers it belongs on the whole to the upper-brackets of street design—Avenues, Promenades, Boulevards, and the like. The big stuff. The two main streets of Perugia, for instance, with their rival variations on the theme, *gradient*. 51 is convex and boldly curving, acknowledging the earth's roundness, also its capacity to roll on and over the edge, thus forcing the visitor upward to find out what happens the other side of the hill (quite a lot in this case). Anticipation. The other, 54, gives the same hill (it really is) the concave treatment. No longer round and rolling but straight and—like Regent Street—ewe-necked, the Via Vanucci presents ant-hill traffic effects which look uncontrived but in fact demand a two-way incline, By going down-hill before it goes up, the traffic climbs above

concave

53
54

itself and is seen to be doing so. The view is from
the steps of the cathedral, the last of its kind we
propose to deal with here, partly because this
is a study in enclosure, and partly because space
exploration is the stuff of conventional town-
planning and has a history and a literature.
Disastrous on the whole, since opening-up in the
name of traffic flow usually succeeds in tearing
away the curtain of mystery native to a good town.
Which is why, when mauled by Sitte's artless
planners, the street often turns out to be the city's
worst friend—how needlessly we discover when we
turn to the work of our predecessors who had no
difficulty in reconciling enclosure and circulation.
But then they had a number of tricks and used
them, beginning with the most important of all

Concave

The Street

55

56

key-hole

definable as the rabbit-warren concept, seen here
in its most primitive form as a hole, rabbit- or key-,
but at Sabbioneta well illustrated in the canyon
effects of the Via Prato Raineri, 135. The
secret lies in treating the street as a *way through*
instead of a through-way by emphasizing the
burrowing rather than the bulldozing nature of
the thing. Once conceived as a *dive* it becomes a
cave, with towering sides which rise up to enclose
it, so introducing a second important concept,
that of the picture frame or

Picture-frame

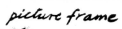

picture frame

57

58

proscenium arch. The street as stage-set.
Important because it establishes a whole
visual philosophy, one the Lazise planners, 57,
were obviously well acquainted with. Look at the
tree, as well placed as the sycamore in the
High at Oxford. No danger of this street blowing
the gaff on the rest of the town either (for what
it has to blow the gaff on turn to page 187).
The house closing the vista could—it doesn't
of course—shut off the circulation entirely, and
so create the equivalent of a back-drop with its

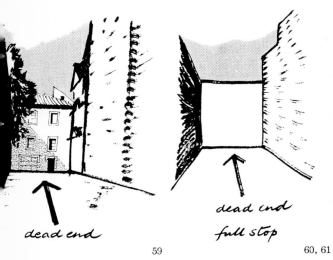

dead end

dead end
full stop

59

60, 61

unpleasing association with a dead-end, the
absolute closure, ultimate way of cutting off all
communications. To get the full weight of the
blow the house barring the way must be in full
elevation, dead square to the viewer, that is.
The smallest touch of perspective defeats the
purpose. One has only to turn the thing through
one degree for the message to shift from, 61,
keep-out-this-means-you to, 62, come-on-in-
and-see-if-we-can't-find-a-way-around-this-
thing-together. Another degree or two

Invitation

62, 63

invitation

deflection 1.

64   65

and the message shifts again, from come-on-in to
look-who's-here. Both eye and mind are delighted
by the change of front, 64. The element of doubt has
been removed, the way through is no longer in
question. Thus, in lieu of fighting a rearguard
action for the feet, the eye is ready to relax and
enjoy the scene, grateful now for something else,
the chopping up of the linear network into a
visually digestible slice of town. Pedestrianly

digestible as well. The promise of more round the
next bend would lead normally to anticipation,
but here the self-importance of the building, and
its favoured position in the line of sun and
vision, create a mental closure on top of the
physical one so that between here and there the
feet enjoy a state of euphoria. One of the
townscaper's highest achievements, inducing
euphoria in the feet. A few degrees more and the

deflection 2

66   67

situation alters again. The change of direction
here is so slight and so polite as to leave one
totally unprepared for what's waiting just
around the corner (one of Foligno's most
splendid squares), 66. When the moment comes
the modesty of the deflection, just enough to
close the street end, no more, heightens the
shock. A two-way closure. The angle is just
enough to bar the street-end and also just enough

deference

to prevent the square-basher getting any but an oblique view back down it. In the cause of stopping leaks a routine frequently resorted to when the T-trap isn't available. His eye—instead of following the line of the roadway to infinity— is brought up all standing on the house-frontages one side.

The same result—self-closure—follows when the whole street lists—to port in the case of 69, an example of what might be called *deference* to the pompous structure on the left, which thus becomes a focal point without prejudice to the street alignment. It seems to be centred while staying just where it is, on the side. Oddly enough the opposite exercise which might be called

68

69

Indeference

indeference

indeference, a distrustful edging-away, realizes the same result—the unpopular party still remains the focus of interest. But where both sides of the street list and list inwardly

Narrows

72, 73

a head-on crash is threatened with results that suck one through the closing door with a force as relentless as that which does the same thing to a cat. Actually one side or the other generally has the sense to give way and this leads to the most favoured of all Italian townscape ploys—the resort to

Wings

74, 75

Wings, used in the sense the word is used in the theatre—out of which the practice may well have stepped. Embryonic here, but rapidly assuming a dominant role

76, 77

wings 2.

as a way of ringing the changes on street width, or, conversely, creating small piazzas—object always the same, *enclosure*—until the moment arrives when the wing

78, 79

wings 3

itself occupies so much of the stage as practically to stop the show so that we are nearly back with the dead-end. Not quite though, 79. There are endless variations, from

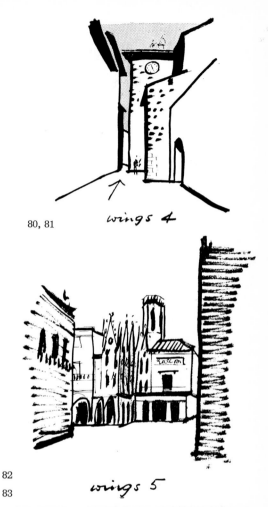

80, 81

the humble stepped narrows, highly congested,
with a delightful un-axial use of the tower, 80, to the
full blown civic composition, 83, again occupying
so much of the available space as to graduate
from side-screen to stage-set, including back-
cloth, though in fact a large main street gets
through. A particularly engaging variation, also
hailing from the stage, though next to
impossible to photograph, is the inclined wing,
which may start as a chamfered corner, 84, but
quickly develops a functional meaning in its own

wings 4

wings 5

82
83

84, 85

wings 6

86, 87

wings 7

right by identifying itself with any incoming transverse street, 86, and signalling its arrival on the scene in a way to gratify the traffic engineer as well as the planner. The townscaping eye is gratified too by the juxtaposition here of the retreating plane of the Wing (the incoming, overlapping street, 87) with the rectangular projection in the foreground which acts as an advance bastion to the (invisible) square. This is at Iseo. At Brescia, 89, the exercise is repeated in reverse. The transverse street, instead of running away, *approaches* the eye, springs out on it from behind the back of a similar bastion. Again unphotographable but very daring in the round. And done here on a scale which introduces movement into the story so that the invading Wing becomes more part of the drama than a frame

to it. Not its orthodox theatrical job which is, basically, to introduce something else, preferably the Set-Piece, the Duomo at Florence here, 91, one of the world's notorious Set-Pieces, yet how many eyes have spotted the Wing that sets the Set-Piece off. Except, perhaps, to revile it as an interloper. One can imagine some artless planner lobbying the local authority to get it pulled down so as to uncover Giotto's tower, the kind of vandalism Mussolini committed, alas, in Rome. Not a single one of the seven approaches to the Duomo at Florence gives more than a partial glimpse of the building, hence its enormous effectiveness as a permanent captive balloon, a likeness heightened by the contrast in materials between it and its neighbours. Breathtaking when floodlit at night, one of Europe's top bits of theatre, repeated in a

88   89

wings 8

90, 91

Set-Piece

set-piece

thereby catching the monument in flank, indeed practically running it down. By artless standards a vast town-planning gaffe, in practice a most acceptable device, surprising the Beloved in an attitude of unconscious grace by precisely the means used to stop her striking one of her poses. Italian towns are full of good buildings like

92

tradesman's entrance

94
95

slightly lower key at Orvieto, but here with an interesting variation involving the main street (the lane in the frontal view, 92, is hardly more than an alley) which arrives, 95, in the Piazza by the back—or anyway side—door,

93

set-piece 2

96, 97

this one at Manciano, 96, which can *only* be got at by
the side door. In consequence they rank less as
buildings than as perspective sculpture, an
important extension of architectural convention
which explains, perhaps, another popular but
extraordinary device, depending for its effect
upon the outrage it arouses in the human breast.
The side door opens—but upon the *corner* of the
building, so that axis and diagonal are, as near
as makes no difference, one. None other, this,
than the

side door

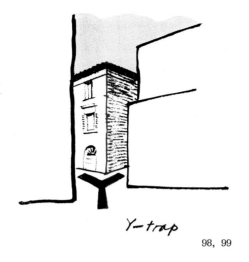

Y-trap

98, 99

100

Y-trap, mentioned already, impressive as a sculptor's dream, deadly as a traffic ploy, so deadly as to turn out rather safe: at such points even Italians have to slow down. The same ploy can be incorporated into the street perspective where by teaming up with our late friend, the stage Wing, the Y achieves the concertina effects of a

Folding Screen

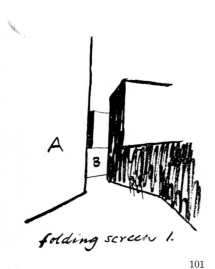

folding screen 1.

101   102

folding screen, seen in 101 and 102, before the concertina effects come into play as no more than a nice piece of urban scenery with an elegantly closed vista. But as the eye advances what appeared to be a conventional piece of street closure, B, is discovered to be something else, a section of the screen, caught now, 103, 104, in the act of folding. Result, the fluctuating wall, to be

103   104

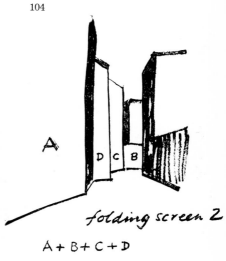

folding screen 2

A + B + C + D

105
106

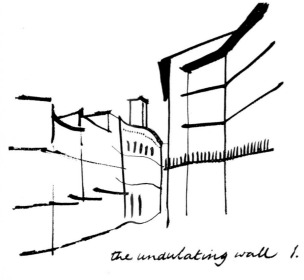

the undulating wall 1.

distinguished from the undulating wall (105, far
distance) by the use of angles against the other's
curves. Both fluctuations and undulations are shewn
here in a very satisfying conjunction, foreground
and background, though again the effect hardly
gets across in the photograph. Fortunately the
artist has caught it brilliantly. Undulations are
generally identified with Baroque impulses
but Italians have used them as stock routines for
centuries. Perugia provides

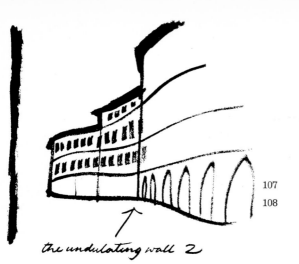

the undulating wall 2

an undulating wall, 108, on quite a monumental scale. Deliberate obviously, but also quite unforced, the quintessence of good townscape, and, again, like the folding screen, having the properties of the Wing in achieving closure. Barring two periods when the vogue was for the straight line it is difficult to find an Italian street which doesn't.

107

108

Undulating Wall

The Street

109

Street Arcades

No accident that most of the analogies so far
have been theatrical ones. With 110 and 111 there
can be no more doubt about it, we have walked
straight on to the stage. What's more, the curtain's
up and the scene set for Montagues and Capulets,
or, rather, mummers and mystery players—they
performed in the street in the middle ages with
consequences almost certainly fruitful for
townscape. Evidence that the builders thought
in terms of stage effects is provided by the
arcades' enormous height, for in general arcading
in sunspot towns is kept low, 112, to crowd out
hot air and bright light.

110   111

Besides its properties as background the arcade has two compelling townscape virtues, the first of which—its capacity to create and multiply perspectives, 109, 110, 111—furnishes the lucky citizen with the nice-dream essentials of adventure (the rabbit hole again) and safety (by enclosure). Ordinarily the eye has too many responsibilities for comfort—safety, protection, defence, contacts, food, orientation, opportunity, pleasure and the job of boxing the compass. Result, fatigue, mostly unconscious. By the extent to which it reduces the eye's commitments by limiting and canalizing the visual possibilities, arcading does a lot to relieve the pressure. Hence the warm and womb-like sense of comfort one experiences in such streets.

112

114

115

Neon

The argument against arcading in England
revolves around the amount of daylighting
lost to the shop-keeper, a valid consideration
before electricity in general and neon in particular
revolutionized, 115, the urban scene. When you
remember that a majority of urban days in a
Northern latitude are wet or grey or foggy and
demand artificial lighting anyway, and weigh the
disadvantage of premature lighting against the
advantage of a protected pavement where the
pedestrian can afford to window-shop at leisure
without the interference of the elements, the dice
seem to be loaded in favour of the arcade. That,
anyway, was how they saw it in Bologna, 113, 114,
built, remember, against the Northern rains rather
than the Southern suns.

116

Pavement Life

Final argument for the arcade, the opportunities it offers—116, a scene at Assisi—for pavement life. It is the absence of pavement-café society that accounts for the lack of civic warmth in English urban life, due, these days anyway, more to lack of initiative than unkind weather. The roof looks after the rain, glass screens can take care of the wind, underfloor heating would finish the job. As to the fog, for the pedestrian in an arcaded city, protected by piloti and dazzled by an Aurora Borealis of disembodied neon, fog is a revelation. Bologna can be hotter, colder, wetter, windier and foggier than London yet, in the main, beats the elements at the game. It makes great use of pavement cafés and glass screens and on a foggy day becomes an enchanted city. Anyone who has not been in Bologna in a fog cannot be said to know what true urban felicity is.

The Street

The Townscape Tradition

Street, like *City*, is almost a dirty word today. Street boy, street walker, on the streets, from the streets. Hard indeed it is for refugees from the industrial revolution to reconstruct an urban world of such allure that its earlier escapologists, the puritans, compared it to a fair. A particularly plushy one. No one in his senses even thought of getting out. Except, like Pilgrim, to save his virtue, flying from Vanity Fair as from some lush doll lest he be debauched by her charms.

The sixty-four thousand dollar question now comes up, were those charms natural or artificial? Did the idea of a planned ensemble, matching gold eye-shadow, finger nails, bag, gloves, stilettos, costume jewellery, enter into the doll's stream of consciousness, or was the final product in all its finery as accidental as a hornbill's tail feather?

For the ordinary citizen the answer seems obvious. Towns *grew*. The medieval city was a picturesque jumble and a picturesque jumble is the opposite of a plan. His view is based on a naïve thought sequence which identifies order with system and system with symmetry. Where there is no symmetry there is no order, the argument runs, and—man being a rational animal—where there is disorder absence of conscious direction must be inferred. Hence Filarete's Sforzinda is town-planning (it was in fact a piece of wizard-of-ozardry) while picturesque medieval muddle is the product of 'natural causes'.

Modern planning theory with its emphasis on functional issues repudiates the symmetrical fallacy. It reminds the plain citizen that the original meaning of symmetry in the Greek was balance, a very different thing, and the balances in many medieval towns were often wonderfully adjusted. Because their build-up is organic rather than rational it doesn't follow that

77

the emerging pattern or lack thereof must be accidental. This theme the student of organism can go along with quite smoothly so long as he avoids the mistake of turning for corroboration to the literature of town-planning, for when he does he finds there isn't any. Virtually no literature, literally no corroboration, and such literature as there is echoes the plain citizen's sentiments, not his, with Budgy-like fidelity. Almost to a man from the father of Philosophy onwards those who have jumped into print on the subject have treated it as the art of creating the ideal town and the ideal town is *never* a picturesque muddle. It is on the contrary strictly symmetrical, standing on absolutely level ground (Cicero) with gridiron plan divided into twelve parts each with its particular Temples, Chapels, square Squares, and wide straight noble streets, these handsomely paved and beautifully contrived with public edifices and houses built regularly and in similar style and at uniform height and joined one to another (Babylon's, that unideal city, weren't, by the way) in such a manner that the whole city will have the form of a single building, thus amongst other things providing the town with a wall (Plato). Alberti (failing us for once) adds that houses will be rendered much more noble if the doors are built all after the same model.

The gridiron sometimes gave way to the Catherine Wheel, but the symmetrical ideal remained unchanged. For us, who live in a gridiron world without finding it particularly ideal, it is difficult to understand why the prophets of town-planning argued in these terms until the realization dawns that though they may have been prophets they were not prophets of town-planning but doctors of philosophy, hailing, almost to a man, from the Platonic cornbelt, a prairie if ever there was one. And home of prairie plans, each little more than a three-dimensional allegory of the good life, hence their appalling dullness—Plato, you will remember, wouldn't even let foreigners into town lest they corrupt the citizenry.

Add to the doctors of philosophy a few wizards and a sprinkling of mad military engineers and even madder princelings with an urge to reconcile building and ballistics, and you have about all history can offer on the subject between the fall of Rome and the sixteenth century. And when towns with systematic layouts do reappear their new regularity does more than encourage the plain citizen in his faith, it convinces him that Cinquecento builders held a view of town-planning similar to his, as the art of getting symmetry into picturesque muddle.

Nor on this point would the historians disagree with him. Here is where the functional planner begins to see that he has been tricked into something dangerously like a regress. By defining it as the business of regularizing muddle his opponent is able to deny the existence of planning except when the formal pattern he fancies turns up. To break this vicious circle a new work-out on picturesque muddle seems indicated and here the student of organism has had a stroke of luck, for there is, as it happens, a modern parallel to the picturesque and muddled medieval cities in the picturesque and muddled English landscape. Is this, too, the product of 'natural causes'? Yes, indeed, the plain citizen would answer, insofar as agriculture is a natural cause, and insofar as its picturesqueness shows it to be unplanned.

This time, however, he would not find the historians so accommodating. Picturesque it certainly is, but not unplanned. In the history of art no picture has been more deliberately painted, down to the last dead tree, yet the fact that this accidental looking landscape was the work of thousands of highly self-conscious amateur 'improvers' had been overlooked well before the last of them was a hundred years dead. The rediscovery of their art—landscape gardening—easily the most important art this country has produced—depended largely on the touch-and-go of a flimsy literature, dependent again on the new eighteenth-century fashion of printing and publishing what amounted to private country-house jokes. In their absence, no painting, no picture, no artist, no improver, no conscious direction at all, just the English Countryside, picturesque, muddled, folksy, product of natural causes.

Touch-and-go indeed. The moral doesn't permit us to claim the same history for the picturesque muddle of the Middle Ages. It does reinforce the reasonable view that if they were not in the modern sense 'planned' (meaning grimly bye-lawed) the medieval towns were most certainly *made* with all the prodigality of the creative spirit. And with eyes alive to the pattern. Contrived, as they used to say. Which suggests that if town-planning (in the current sense) is a new development, townscape is an old one. Which again suggests that our ancestors were a bit more subtle than we give them credit for. And a bit more successful. Every generation believes itself to be the first beneficiary of full self-consciousness, thereby tacitly denying that distinction to its predecessors. Ours is not an exception. Yet even in the absence of direct proof it seems a reasonable bet that the intuitions of men who made nice towns come a bit nearer the essence and inner meaning of town-planning than does the exact science of those who, like ourselves, make vile ones.

There is a valid retort to this. If they were indeed our betters at the game how comes it that our ancestors, when they did turn to formal planning, could surface with nothing more interesting than Dürer's grid or More's Utopia? The answer is equally valid. Because from first to last, from Dürer to Christianopolis, the mess of pottage we are being served up with on plate after plate is still the ideal city—more pie-in-the-sky from more philosophers waving Utopian blueprints that are still nothing better than the doodles of do-gooders. To make a true appreciation one would need to find a ready-made real-life town of the right period and analyse its effects in three dimensions on the spot, not an easy assignment obviously since ready-made towns of the right period do not grow on trees. But suppose the real thing did turn up. And suppose the pattern turned out to combine two kinds of logic, formal and picturesque (the townscape equivalent of Brunelleschi's San Spirito), then two complementary conclusions could be justifiably drawn. The men of the Renaissance could be accepted as heirs of a *living* planning tradition and the picturesque muddle of the Middle Ages could be put down to more deliberate purposes than 'natural causes'. Concede the possibility of *picturesque planning** and the whole situation changes. In places of accidental muddle on the one hand and conscious town-planning on the other, a choice could be made between two complementary townscape approaches, formal and informal, symmetrical and asymmetrical, regular and irregular, classic and romantic, rational and organic, free and formal.

But where is one going to find this text-book example? Just to start off with, if the cry later interpolations is not to be heard ringing through its streets the town in question will have to be guaranteed designed and built at the drop of a hat. Only the first condition, that. Of those that do satisfy it there are not more than two of the right date in all Italy and it would surely be over-sanguine to expect either of these to oblige. Or would it? Believe it or not one of them does, Sabbioneta, a city-statelet belonging to the Princes of Mantua and situated some twenty miles from that town. Built between 1550 and 1564 by Vespasian Gonzaga, a man of violent energy and ferocious temper (he kicked his son to death), Sabbioneta provides (it is suggested here) conclusive evidence not only that town-planning was a well digested science in the sixteenth century but that townscape—picturesque townscape—was in an advanced state of development and practised by self-conscious operators.

Before this proposition is turned down with the contempt it deserves let us add that the theme is not an entirely novel one. Sitte was convinced as early as 1889 that much of the picturesque muddle of Italian and, indeed, other European towns—the hambone shapes of squares, for instance, and

* Free planning is the current term, an exercise sometimes treated as a side-kick of functionalism and replaced here for that reason, because *Picturesque* has visual and historical associations the other lacks and is thus able to integrate free planning with its own tradition.

the tangental impulses of streets—was far from accidental. In that belief
he analysed about a hundred European *plazas* with highly interesting
results. There is another piece of literary evidence even better than Sitte's,
Alberti's, written (though not published) around 1450 and in the context of
the case we are discussing, immensely significant since Alberti and the
Gonzagas were hand in glove. It was for Lodovico III that Alberti in 1470
designed the church of Sant' Andrea, Mantua, at which Court he was an
honoured guest. Not, it is true, in the company of Vespasian, who was of a
later generation, but doubtless selling the whole family, present and future,
his act as the Florentine Vitruvius. The Roman original Vespasian is known
to have treated as his private bible and carried with him to the wars and it
isn't stretching credibility far to believe the new Vitruvius was in the Glad-
stone bag as well, though the two works would hardly have made good bed-
fellows—Alberti regarded his model as a dimwit who couldn't write his
mother tongue and said so in no uncertain words.*

To the ideal Platonic tradition we have already discussed Alberti is
virtually the one exception. Here we have that rare phenomenon, an architect of the highest genius with a brilliant literary talent. In consequence,
perhaps, a crack appears in the uninviting paste-board walls of the ideal
city and a small piece of townscape grins through. Only a small piece but
when one considers it in relation to Sabbioneta and the Gonzaga link, a very
significant one indeed. Thinking (also perhaps significantly of precisely the
kind of miniature town Sabbioneta was, and is), Alberti says:

'But if it is only a small town, or a fortification, it will be better, and as
safe, not for the streets to run straight to the gates; but to have them wind
about sometimes to the right, sometimes to the left, near the wall, and
especially under the towers upon the wall; and within the heart of the
town it will be handsomer not to have them strait, but winding about
several ways, backwards, and forwards, like the course of a river. For
thus, besides that by appearing so much the longer, they will add to the
idea of the greatness of the town, they will likewise conduce very much to
beauty and convenience, and be a greater security against all accidents
and emergencies. Moreover, this winding of the streets will make the
passenger at every step discover a new structure, and the front and door
of every house will directly face the middle of the street; and whereas in

* '. . . he [Vitruvius] wrote in such a manner, that to Latins he seems to write Greek,
and to Greeks, Latin: But indeed it is plain from the book itself that he wrote neither
Greek nor Latin, and he might almost as well have never wrote at all, at least with regard
to us, since we cannot understand him.' Book VI of Alberti's *Dei Libri*, chap. 1, p. 111,
in the English edition (Tiranti).

larger towns even too much breadth is unhandsome and unhealthy, in a small one it will be both healthy and pleasant, to have such an open view from every house by means of the turn of the street.

'But further; in our winding streets there will be no house but what, in some part of the day, will enjoy some sun; nor will they ever be without gentle breezes which, whatever corner they come from, will never want a free and clear passage; and yet they will not be molested by stormy blasts, because such will be broken by the turning of the streets. Add to all these advantages that, if the enemy gets into the town, he will be in danger on every side, in front, in flank, and in rear, from assaults from the houses. So much for the publick streets. The private ones should be like the publick, unless there be this difference, that they be built exactly in strait lines, which will answer better to the corners of the building, and the divisions and parts of the houses.

'The ancients in all towns were for having some intricate ways and turn-again streets, without any passage through them, that if an enemy comes into them he may be at a loss, and be in confusion and suspence; or if he pushes on daringly, may be easily destroyed. It is also proper to have smaller short streets, running across from one street to another; not to be as a direct publick way, but only as a passage to some house that fronts it; which will both give light to the houses, and make it more difficult for an enemy to over-run all parts of the town.'

The requirements of defence in passages like this are used rather as they are by politicians today, as a pretext for doing what you want to do. 'Even when', writes S. Lang of Alberti (in by far the best short account of the history of town planning that has yet appeared),* 'he pretends utilitarian considerations, his real concern is obviously with aesthetic questions.' Sabbioneta doesn't exactly *wind*, but that's the interesting thing. Without exactly winding it does manage to carry out all Alberti's ideals for a small town even down to 'turn-again streets' and 'intricate ways'. On the surface the plan is as the guide books and scholars describe it, star-shaped, formal, grid-ish, fortified, yet not one of these aspects has any real bearing on the end-product which is of an extremely subtle, romantic, synoptic sort, deeply opposed to what is widely regarded as the Cinquecento ideal—the through-way by-passes the town square—T-junctions to all exits—lead-ins—street lengths reduced to a minimum—entrance gates masked—all exits to town masked—all views of the world excluded—no rational

---

* In fact the only one—'The Ideal City' in *The Architectural Review*, August 1952, p. 93.

plan—no quick picture—no geometry—no grasp permitted of the master-plan or underlying rationale—on the contrary, surprise, anticipation, mystery, frustration, chinese boxes, shock, delight, all in the compass of one dusty village exposed upon the flat irrigations of the Po Valley, an area of no mystery, and even less romance.

The plan itself is dealt with in greater but far from exhaustive detail in the illustrations that follow. One need not say more here than that the result demonstrates the existence in the sixteenth century of an aesthetic which is only now being explored in the second half of the twentieth.* Sir Uvedale Price, that ornament of our race, lampooned by Peacock in Headlong Hall and thereafter elbowed out of existence, when quizzed by Repton for his part in the destruction of the traditional English *formal* garden, maintained with passion that to destroy ornamental planting of parterres of box or yew or avenues of elm or chestnut when they were acting as extensions of the house to which they belonged was against every principle of Picturesque *as opposed* to Landscape Theory. Picturesque Theory, he asserted, demands formality where it is justified by the genius loci, and should and could assimilate the Grand Manner *whenever it is picturesquely required*. Whenever, that is, its presence is dictated by the Picturesque aesthetic. A lofty sentiment but one that was never implemented. In the nineteenth century, Picturesque and Beaux Arts routines, the visual philosophies of the two preceding centuries, remained separated by the coldest of cold wars, each chewing its underlip when the other turned up, not to say gnawing the ends of its moustaches. Not till Le Corbusier used them as foils was reconciliation even conceived to be a visual possibility. Yet in point of fact that reconciliation had been effected centuries earlier in the Italy of the CINQUE-CENTO. Such anyway is the contention here. That Cinquecento townscape was founded on what might now be called a picturesque approach to the Grand Manner. Or, if you like, a romantic use of classic principles. Or a free use of the formal. Or a formal interpretation of the organic. Put it what way you like, these are the very issues that exercise the master-minds of our day apropos (on Civilia's narrower front) the relation of space and volume and (on a very much broader) such dicey questions as the possible armistice between science and religion.

---

* Some would argue that townscape of this kind—the employment of formal patterns to romantic ends—was the basis of the later work at Bath, but into that we needn't go now.

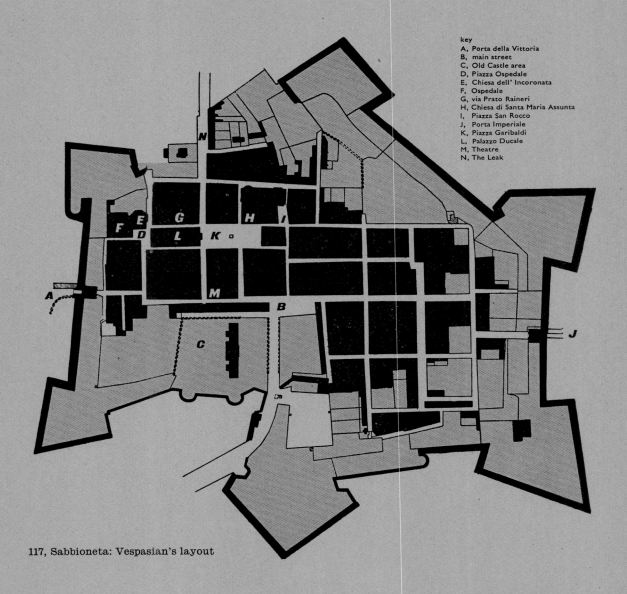

117, Sabbioneta: Vespasian's layout

Palmanova

Up to now the argument has clung round the
neck of one only of the two existing Cinquecento
towns. The other, because it is the first-ever
radial plan, because of the paradox of that
plan's origin, and because of the strange fact that
Scamozzi, who built it in 1593, originally prepared
another, founded, like Sabbioneta, on the grid,
has an equally dramatic history. They are, indeed,
mutually involved. Three years before he built
Palmanova Scamozzi had completed his theatre
at Sabbioneta for Vespasian (M, above) so his

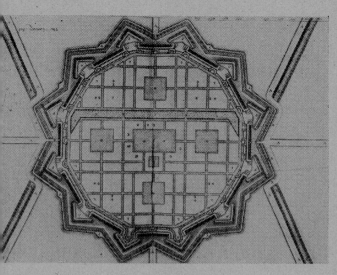

118, Scamozzi's first plan for Palmanova

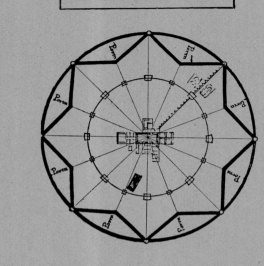

119, Filarete's plan for Sforzinda

familiarity with the town is not in doubt, and though the differences between the two plans are those one might expect of an adroit professional and an amateur of genius, there are enough similarities to establish common ground. Somewhere between one and the other, however, something surprising happened. Lost in an unreadable and unpublished treatise dedicated to one of the Sforzas of Milan—hence its name—a New Look was born. It rustled through all the Courts of Europe and sometime before 1593 came to Scamozzi's knowledge. He fell for it and the fall was a fateful one: it sparked off a fresh spate of ideal towns, radial this time, starting but, alas, not ending with Palmanova itself.

Where lies the paradox? To appreciate it one must first repeat after Pevsner the creed of the radial plan, much more than a new gimmick, this, a confession of faith, a confession of humanist faith, with everything above the belt dedicated to Man, the new centre of the universe—and everything below firmly planted in astrology and magic. For the surprising thing that came between Scamozzi and his first and second plans was nothing less than the cartwheel of Sforzinda, 119, and Sforzinda, as Lang has pointed out, was improvised by Filarete, himself a bit of a wizard, out of symbols that belong in the dark waters of medieval magic. Humanism and sorcery,

a strange mésalliance, but only so long as one admits no common ground between Medieval and Renaissance man, the old Adam and the new. Do the other thing, agree that human nature, then as now, had a bit of both Adams, and add that military experts, then as now, were vocal and officious, and one might be on the track of why Sforzinda had so startling a success. Enduring too; disguised as the *Rondpoint* it still survives in the Beaux Arts tradition and Washington, DC; evidence, perhaps, of a marriage of convenience rather than a mésalliance, highly prolific though hardly fruitful.

The point of the story is that both Palmanova, 118, and Sabbioneta, 117, demonstrate the existence prior to the new, dull epidemic of ideal townage, of a Renaissance concept more subtle and elastic than that which superseded it. Their own superficially rigid geometry gives evidence of *picturesque intention*, meaning in this context an impulse to create the sort of cosy and self-sealing environment which provides the real charms of urban living, and to that extent suggests another such marriage of convenience between Medieval and Renaissance ideas—a marriage this time of the old know-how to the new concept. An important consideration for the townscaper (as we have seen) because, by presupposing an old know-how it encourages him to claim a pre-Renaissance

85

120, Scamozzi's second plan for Palmanova, an air view

history for his art and so a place in the sun for its greatest tour de force, the medieval city. At present the position is the one architecture would occupy were all that preceded Michelangelo, that alarming natural phenomenon, expunged from the slate. The sensible conclusion seems to be Sitte's, that men like Vespasian were tapping a townscape vein worked in earlier days and not yet exhausted. Thus what at first appeared to be a standard Cinquecento grid turns into an exercise in Alberti's advice to dissemble. Main instrument and symptom of this intention, the T-crossing— since it is used to bamboozle the eye as to the master-plan hereafter called the T-trap. And given special emphasis in this discussion because it lends itself to illustration where other nuances do not. The number of such T-traps the artist was able to uncover before exhaustion intervened in an area of two major and some nine or ten minor streets is shown in 121. There are as well L-, P-, and U-traps, quads, courts, cul-de-sacs and cosy corners, all arranged on the maze principle to disguise the real lay-out of the town, basically quite an elementary one, as that of so small a place would have to be. Palmanova's is both more pretentious and less subtle but the T-traps are there and, as G. A. Jellicoe has suggested, the streets and open spaces have a variety of proportion which would build up well in three dimensions. This promising start was now nipped in the bud by Sforzinda and the second Palmanova, 120, mere clichés by comparison—the first artless plans in modern European history, to be follow-my-leadered by an exhausting procession of equally artless cartwheels and grids. Now and then, when the Grand Manner coughed up a man of genius,

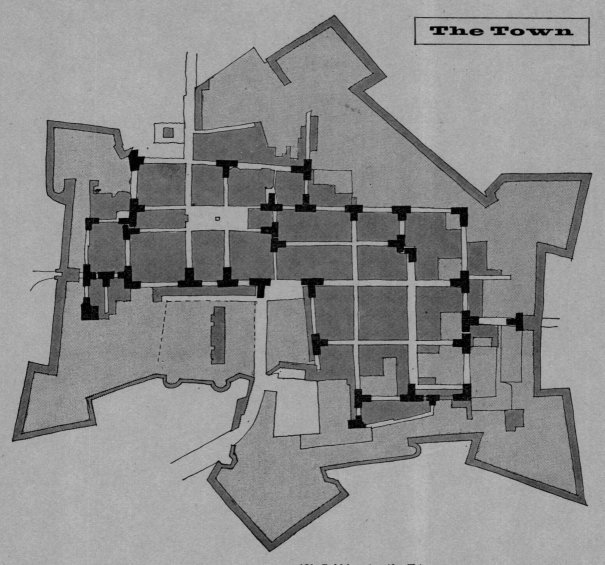

121, Sabbioneta: the T-traps

something dodgy came up but, mainly, the trend
of four centuries has been to foster a theory of
town-planning so outrageously over-simplified
as to be disastrous to urban man, second in its
capacity for disruption, indeed, only to the industrial
revolution. The coup de grace has been delivered
in our own day by internal combustion, a form of
artillery which found artless plans very much
to its liking—you could shoot straight—and in
combination the three set up that process of chain
fission which has completed the dismemberment
of the city.

Sabbioneta : the scene

The Porta Vittoria was built by Vespasian in 1562. The inscription above it records the event. Within yards of entering it, 123, one is faced with a T-junction which involves both a change of direction and a decision as to which direction to take. Yet the main street is only just around the corner—why the diversion? The evidence supports beyond all reasonable doubt a deliberate intention to blindfold the stranger at the gate so that the town and its shape shall not be immediately apparent to him. The reasons, aesthetic rather than military, Alberti's intricate ways; the concealing of the master plan.

122

123

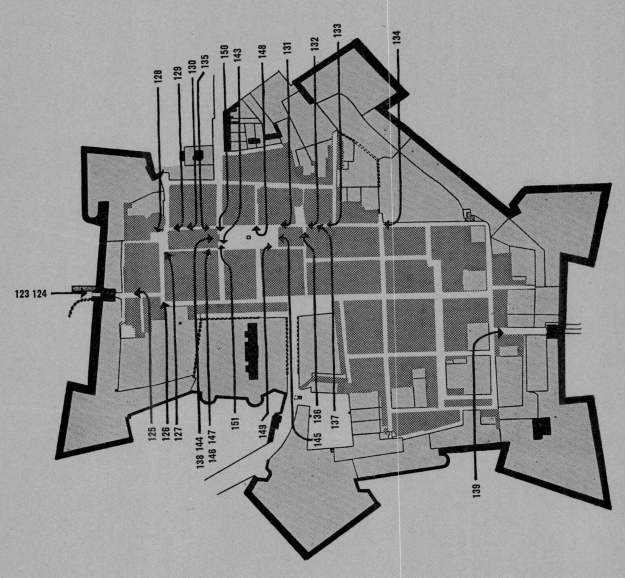

88

, 125

It may be accident but when you pass through the
archway and look back, 125, the same thing
happens, this time in the extra-mural world, which
is effectively bunkered by a timely obstruction
involving a road deflection. Not even by a glance
is the citizen allowed to know the scene is set in
the middle of a vast plain. It is, however, and the
contrast heightens the massive sense of enclosure
within the Gates. The scroll over the archway, 124,
celebrates Vespasian's erection in 1562 of this noble
piece of stage scenery, 'borrowed' by Gerolamo
Cattameo from Mantua (and Giulio Romano).
In the sequence which follows, the pedestrian in 126
plays a useful walking-on part (no lines). He has
come from the Porta della Vittoria and would be
heading into the awning seen through the archway
in 123 had he not decided to turn left to the Ospedale
where we shall follow him. The camera catches him
in the act of turning.

We come now to a startling series of shocks.
Following the pedestrian up the street the eye is
met by the Campanile of the octagonal Chiesa
dell'Incoronata, E and 126, a section of its dome
and one bay and a half of its portico, the first
intimation we are given of the presence of the
Piazza Ospedale, D. Very charming too, 127, exactly
the proportions one would expect of the town
square except that it isn't the town square. As
one soon finds, it is a take-in. From this point
on the camera moves backwards. Before doing
likewise please take a look, 135, at what is coming
up. Here, in the remarkable scene which meets the
eye as one pulls out of the Piazza, utterly unprepared
after that bright little interlude for a canyon
which makes a gash through the whole length of
the town, G, not much over four hundred yards
really but a frightening distance to the eye.
S. Maria Assunta, H, you will notice, is not allowed
any projections that might get in the way of the
gash and for a good reason, lest suspicions be
aroused in promenading breasts as to its real
function as the Big Wheel of the Piazza Garibaldi.
Why? Because the very existence of the Piazza
Garibaldi is being kept from promenading breasts by
townscaper Vespasian. As of now it is the gash that
matters, nothing else, and in order that the street
may be sealed good and proper, even from the Piazza
Ospedale, the return wall of the loggia has
been carried across its (the street's) whole width,
129, thus introducing a screen between street and
square. Neither in consequence is revealed to the
other until the last moment when they explode
on the attention, one way (opposite to ours) as a
blaze of sun and air, the other, as a dive into the
dark. And in each case the sense of enclosure
is so strong that one has the feeling of being
lost in the jungle, quite a feat on the planner's
part when you think of the size of the town.
From the Ospedale door, we start to back,
first along the loggia, 128, then sidestepping into
the street, closed now by the loggia's retaining
wall, 129. As we retreat the Ospedale door
continues to vanish, 130, until we are well and truly
trapped in the canyon. Later, townscaper
Vespasian's purpose in all this by-play is
revealed in the determined way in which the
campanile of Incoronata closes the vista, 130, 131,
132. At one point, 131, by moving a yard sideways
this way or that, we can see a corner of the ducal
palace, a campanile, a monumental church tower
(beheaded in the photograph) and a dome (seen
in 145 right-handed of the column). Thrown
together—accidentally it would seem—they form
the sort of monumental free-for-all, one big boy

93

elbowing the other, that one associates with a
capital city. And Sabbioneta *is* a capital—
Vespasian's—and Vespasian lets you know it by
arranging this impressive back-drop to the palace.
What happens when his bluff is called we shall
see later. Meanwhile, having by-passed in the
interests of one story at a time the Piazza
Garibaldi, we come, instead, to the arcade 132, 137,
which introduces another church, S. Rocco, in
another pint-sized piazza, 136, and repeats, for the
benefit of hither-side visitors, the performance of
the previous one in falsifying the scale (or, rather
establishing the real scale falsified by Garibaldi).
Acts, that is, as a similar bamboozle and take-in.

The Town

138

In any other case than a custom-built town made to
the order of one customer, the tailor himself, one
could hardly speak with such certainty, but here
behind every ploy we have a right to assume
deliberate intention. Thus only once in the whole
of the canyon's journey are we allowed even a
glimpse of the rest of Sabbioneta. All other openings
are T-trapped until, as per Alberti's instructions,
the Via Prato Raineri, G, runs up under the town
wall (so adding several cubits to its stature) before
itself being trapped, 134, and made to take the last
long leg back to the Gate the other end, J, the Porta
Imperiale, 139.

When the Piazza Garabaldi, K and 138, does come
into the picture the reason both for the gash and for
the lesser piazzas is revealed—surprise. Ideal foils,
the gash and the piazzas, deliberate scale-reducers,

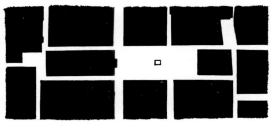

140

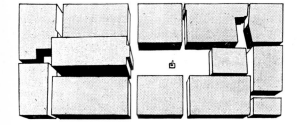

141

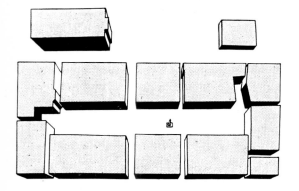

142

143

*140 shows the real area of the Piazza Garibaldi. By
making the left hand end-block higher and the right
hand end-block lower than the surrounding skyline
Vespasian gave them the effect, 141, of separate
buildings, standing in a square, twice its actual size,
142. What are in fact streets entering awkwardly at
Garibaldi's corners he thus transformed, 144, 145,
into the flanks of the greater piazza.*

designed to unprepare you for outsize Garibaldi,
Not all the finer points can be discussed here,
but there is one so Italian, this time in its subtlety,
that it can hardly be ignored. Sitte and Gibberd and
the diagrams on page 209 reveal the impossible
predicament forced on the planner when two street
apertures are required at one corner. Vespasian
had four at two, 140, and took steps to cure the lateral
leak by projecting the palace stair across the
aperture, adding two man-size bollards for good
measure, 143. Remarkably successful they are too.
His main tactic, however, was something much
bolder. Not without difficulty, if the odd super-
structure, 145, is anything to go by, he caused the
Palace to tower above its neighbours in such a
way as to suggest that it, the Palace, like the
Duomo at Florence, is just another of those quart-
size dirigibles, parked in a pint-sized open space.
For photography the point is better made at the
other end of the Piazza, for there Vespasian
repeated the gimmick in reverse, by reducing
instead of increasing the height of the frontage.
Upon this frontage he then clapped a single flattened
roof and, behold, no frontage—instead a charming
little pavilion planted in a quart-sized piazza
whose boundaries, 144, appear (by means
of uniform roof lines and T-traps) to be
extended round the pint-sized pavilion. The
diagram shows what happens. Palace and pavilion,
the large and little captive balloons, not only
give this complex its peculiar sweetness but
conspire to double the Piazza's apparent size.

144

145

The Town

We now come to the moment of truth. Of the four openings to the piazza shown here, three, 148, 149 and 150, are smoothly T-trapped. Result, impressive urban effects. So far so good. But by an accident which can only be guessed at one of the eight possible leaks in the square has been unstopped or never sealed. The result, highly farcical, blows the whole card-castle, with its beautiful Gonzaga illusion of Empire, as flat as the surrounding landscape. Hardly believing his eyes the deceived viewer glares first at the stirring urban scene made up by S. Maria Assunta and the Palazzo, Ducale, 147, and then at the dusty country lane, 151, with wired fences and saplings which comes between. Looking one way, 150, across the Palace steps, Empire, the other, the cruel reality, laid bare for all to see. End of the deception, but it was good while it lasted.

The final point has been made already. Except for the palace not one of the main buildings is either centred or made a centre. The Chiesa dell'Incoronata, E, has nothing but its campanile on the axis of any thoroughfare. Its dome is always seen off-centre. S. Maria Assunta, H, is neither centrally placed in the Piazza nor on the axis of one of the entering streets. The theatre, M, is on a corner. The Via Prato Raineri, G, hugs one side of

the town as does the Piazza Garibaldi itself. The T-trap is everywhere. This is no grid. It isn't even formal planning. It is picturesque planning clothed in formal dress. Scamozzi's first plan for Palmanova has many points in common, the T-trap in particular, though here one can feel the weakening of old techniques as the Grand Manner throws its shadow before. The moral? Surely, that the European planning tradition is picturesque. Free planning, far from being a novelty, has a long history stemming from the middle ages. The counter-measures of philosophers, military engineers, eccentrics like Filarete, megalomaniacs like Louis—the whole French nation, indeed, with its passion for *gloire*, so boringly interpreted in the Beaux Arts canon— occupy an important position in the history of the Opposition but do not represent Civilia's governing impulse. The issue is, perhaps, less one between emotion and reason than a matter of calculation regarding the mind's capacities as a draughtsman —some seeing it as the father and mother of all symmetry, others seeing those who so see it as artless—Sitte's artless planners—underestimators of the reason's capacity for any mathematics higher than simple Euclidian geometry.

5

The Italian Tradition

For races north of the Alps HF, the literary parent of SF, has typed the Italian as the Man behind the Arras. Every schoolgirl with Sir Walter Scott in her satchel learns to recognize the fine Italian hand, the jewelled knife, the poisoned cup, the deep-laid plot, the curious work of art.

In fact the cloak-and-dagger aspect of the Italian personality is in the nature of—hardly a veneer—a compensation for an entirely different kind of character, who may or may not be dangerous, but is most certainly passionate, impatient, violent, above all direct. The converse of the man in the satchel. That passionate directness, the grasping of life at first- not second-hand was the thing that glued Henri Beyle to his window at Civitavecchia. Beside it the façadism of the French and British seemed tedious, as it did, and does, to the Italian, whose natural bonhomie is tested by the impatience he feels of the tergiversators.

Impatience. The complement of passionate directness. Its products spread far and wide over the Italian scene, explaining many apparently wayward decisions. And consequences. In the field of townscape, for example, why no monument is ever plumb on an axis or building scheme quite finished. Brunelleschi's dome still lacks collar and tie, Perugia's *Centro* remains in its underpants. In Rome at the top of the Spanish Steps Benedict XIII, Pius VI and the Trinita dei Monti each in turn shrug hardly perceptible shoulders at the others' alignment.

One could go on indefinitely. The cause here springs from a vast contempt for the pedantry of the drawing-board and a still vaster indifference to business efficiency, correspondence, procedures, schedules, dead-lines, the

153, 154

preoccupation, these, of lesser minds. In monumental architecture the form it takes is a strong objection to parallel lines, museum example, the Piazza of S. Mark's with its abutting buildings and open spaces, 155, where Frederick Gibberd has been able to find no parallel lines at all. As one of the results, S. Mark's itself glares directly at the opposite *corner* of the square. In petty detail, likewise, the piazza is sublimely indifferent to axes. Notice the unaxial position of the columns in the Piazzetta, 153, then the extraordinary position of the lamp-posts in relation to the floor pattern, 154, which appears to have been designed to bring the columns back into the picture, until the last round-up, 156, establishes a near miss.

So what? The thing is in the target area, isn't it? Impatience, easy boredom, contempt for pedantic detail, an attitude to pomp and circumstance so casual as to border again on contempt, these scarcely add up to the kind of picture one would expect of the world's greatest builders. Yet, paradoxical as it is, Architecture with a capital A has always remained a top dressing in the country of its supreme triumphs.

Nor has Roman engineering taken its place. At the least provocation the motifs peel off to reveal what lies below the surface—architectonics—a violent preoccupation with fundamental forms in one, two, or three dimensions. Cones, cubes, cylinders, the line, the circle, the square. An elemental geometry expressed in a vernacular of power to which, like Bernini, the greater Italian architects returned from time to time for a wash-and-brush-up.

No class distinctions. The impulse is as clearly isolated in those defence-mechanism status symbols, the Palazzos, founded as they are on the rock—

or rusticaions—of the functional tradition, as in the vernacular of the peasantry. All-purpose too. It could come to the aid of the Faith, 152, or control (with rewarding and ruthless economy) a rush of blood to the head in the shape of the watch-towers which shot up like beanstalks all over the country in the thirteenth century. And stayed up, even when, as at Bologna, 386, leaning over backwards to come down. More defence-mechanism according to the form book, though an observer as shrewd as Alberti saw how thin an explanation that was. He called it something else, a General Infection, 'a kind of General Infection of building high Watch Towers, even in the meanest villages, insomuch that scarce a common house-keeper thought he could not be without his turret: by which means there arose a perfect Grove of Spires'. Impatience again.

There are, of course, dozens of ways of looking at Italian architecture. We are concentrating here on one and only one because despite Nikolaus Pevsner* it seems to have had a poorer press than the others. Since space is short, rather than try to argue it further, let us take one concrete example, a celebrated piece of Baroque, Bernini's Peristyle, and see what that has to say about the business. An odd selection this may seem to anyone who chooses to ignore what has been said above, but unless it is going to discover significant form where Cézanne and the Cubists (not to mention Clive Bell) long ago unearthed it, the operation has got to aim a bit higher than the vernacular. The obligation is upon us to uncover the fundamentalist urge amongst five-star jobs and top people.

Well, nothing could be more five-star than the Peristyle. Nor any Person more totally Top than Bernini. There is a tradition that a colonnade stretched in Roman times from the Tiber to St Peter's or its site. If so, it is fair to say it must have been a very different article from his. Ignoring the baths and greater works of engineering which are mostly late one is always surprised how mean in scale as well as vulgar in execution the run-of-the-

* In *An Outline of European Architecture* (Penguin Books). Pevsner also notes the Italian talent for using, Mannerist fashion, architectural volume as a weapon of spatial exploration.

156

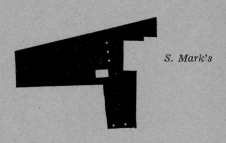

S. Mark's

155 *A silhouette plan of the Piazza*

157

mill Roman work is, from local triumphal arches to the flats at Ostia or the pip-squeak monuments along the Appian Way. The garden-ornament of Hadrian's villa is typical, recalling Lutyens at his Tyringham worst. Such may or may not have been the St Peter's colonnade, a very different affair anyway to Bernini's, the essence of which is the knock-out punch. In plan

and effect it does admittedly echo the austere internal glades of the Coliseum (the ellipse, like *Abbacchio al forno*, might be called a Roman speciality) but where one is a bonus on utility engineering the other is a purposeful and fierce hunting down of a specific aesthetic idea, 157–58, no practical purpose served. The serial arcade, the serialization lying in the repetition of the columnar effect, the arch being left flat. The spectator being left flat too, knocked out by an endless succession of right and left hooks based on the peri in the peristyle. Prize-fighting, this, not boxing. No fancy footwork, no ducking, weaving and stabbing out of straight lefts. Just one tremendous haymaker after another coming from the same place and aimed at the same place, the eye. Before both are closed take a good look at the face behind the fist, no water-front toughie as it turns out, quite another number, well-spoken and full-bottom-wigged, handing out the punishment with the compliments of one violent man-of-the-world to another. And that's the essence of it, urbane violence, the very attar of the rose, button upon the cap, of civilization, with the artist himself in such control of the fight as to be able to judge precisely where to pile on or let up the pressure. Inside the colonnade no quarter. All the fun and games and boys and girls hoisted on to the roof where they are able to keep out of the way and at the same time provide an audience.

About this stagey extravagance there is nothing Roman, much less Classic. It is quintessentially Baroque, and so is the unity of conception. Yet—and this is the point—the devastating nature of the punch is something else again, the Italian in Bernini prevailing over the virtuoso—fundamentalist slapping down Grand Mannerist—with enough gusto to transform a *tour de force* of Papal pageantry into an essay in the functional tradition.

The functionalist tradition. Such a much-more-than-Greek stripping down of the extraneous had no official sanction in the seventeenth century, or, indeed, any other right up to the moment Cubism made of it a cult and functionalism an architectural philosophy. Private sanctions it has always had, however, in the Italian breast, never better expressed than in the illustrations of stairscape, 258-266. Two extremes, the steps and the colonnade, pure utility and pure gimmick, yet both bearing the fundamentalist's stigmata of directness and violence.

6

Objects

The programming of this book parodies the processes of digestion
under which lumps of town, first consumed in huge helpings, are
gradually broken down into smaller more digestible constituents,
until the enquiry arrives at a consideration of elements minute
enough to be received into the system without conscious direction or knowledge. That's the trouble. The small-fry of the urban
scene are widely held to be below professional notice and, like
vitamins, edge their way in unsung, not rating a mention at any
stage of the civic proceedings.

What was said earlier about townscape being the art of re-
alerting the eye to the possibilities of the environment now
becomes a very material issue indeed because about 75 per cent of
all townscape elements are of this under-cover sort; operate below
the level of normal visual consciousness. One means, of course,
townscape consciousness. Most of us *see* the furniture of the street
—traffic signs, cars, hoardings, petrol pumps, shop fascias, stalls,
notices of sale, awnings, railings, lampposts, trees, pavings, post-
boxes, public lavatories, people—as instruments of use or contact,

111

but most of us fail to see them at all in the other sense as the bric-a-brac of our own collective Old—or possibly New—Curiosity Shop. As visuals, that is. Because of this blindness the vast majority of articles of use-about-town have become or remained vile, shapeless or squalid with consequences damaging to the fair face of Civilia.

The cure is to bring them into visual consciousness and so enable them to make their personal impact, to do which the still unre-alerted eye must struggle to see them as *objects* existing in their own right. Significant statements of intention. Articles of choice selected for deliberate display on the larger mantelshelf of the street. The section which follows provides a few examples of this approach, but the whole of the rest of the book consists in fact of variations on the theme, so any beginner who bothers to go on reading beyond this point might, before he does so, find it profitable to give his eye a little lecture on the visual significance of *things*.

Objects

159, 160

Man

Amongst the objects on-stage Man is for obvious
reasons charged with the strongest emotional
over- and under-tones. We start with him,
because though in 'real' life no clean division is
possible it is important here to distinguish
visual—or anyway theatrical—criteria from
humane or moral ones. A picturesque beggar, to
take the obvious example, makes bad social but
good townscape sense. For the former reason the
townscaper may have to do without him, but only
after first exercising his right to regard the
beggar as visual material and nothing else. That
way he is in a position to find an alternative for
the bottom of the Cathedral steps, a way of saying
that the townscape game must be played according
to the rules—more complicated ones than the
painter's, for while moral judgments are
forbidden, dramatic ones are permitted. Men are
not merely forms and colours but specimens as
well, ludicrous, 159, or sinister, 160, with
associations that heighten the emotional
temperature without prejudice to their status as
objects—as visual toys that is, for which the
artist is not morally responsible. Thus the nuns,
161. And the plump lady in the floral pattern. The
nuns are sculpture of a high order, with associations (humility, mercy, chastity)

163
164
161   165

which intensify their significance as townscape.
The plump lady, 162, is simple colour and pattern,
a moving flowerscape in the dull urban
perspective, worthy substitute for the beggar,
indeed worthy substitute for flowers or flower
stall. In this drama, dress obviously has an
important walking-on part and here the townscaper
may not always hold the orthodox view.
Decorative and sinister, Teddy boys ganging up on
the street corner are a pure gift, as are
Spades in zoot-suits and other interesting
departures from the norm, such as winklepickers,
lumber jackets, trail-blazers, jeans, floral shirts,
seaweed hair and sloppy-Jo sweaters. Nor is he
prepared to spit upon grey toppers and hot-house
hats.

162

Movement

Farms distinguish between live- and dead-stock.
Though they don't know it, so do towns. There's
an awful lot of dead-stock in a town, starting
with the rows of cadavers politely called parked
cars, 166, a fact which does much to explain the
pigeon cult. Motion is the most direct reminder
that life is a form of action and pigeons supply
this as well as other less desirable things in
generous quantities. Cars when they consent to
move go faster, but there is an important
distinction between one movement and the other.
The car's insolent refusal to become urbanized
establishes it as an intruder anywhere—everywhere
—in every city—where a perpetual pledge of

its capacity to break out—or through—is
provided by the 'traffic arteries'. Not arteries at
all, in fact, but wounds, through which the life-
blood of the urban thing drains away
together with the foreign bodies that have done
the damage. The contrast between the four-wheeled
ballet whose intention is subversive—to break up
the party—and the feathered world which
aims to make a divertissement while
maintaining a firm resolve to stick around,
highlights the two mobile ideas that are fighting
it out to-day, urban and ex-urban, centripetal
and centrifugal. That the old traffic system
was town-bound and so offered no such challenge
to its parent 163 and 164 admirably show. For

those who want to substitute for sprawl a more civilized life carried out in a more urbane environment which we will call, as opposed to Subtopia, Civilia, the obstinate determination of the pigeons to stay right there in the centre and damn the consequences holds a healthy moral.

168

167

Action

Unlike the pigeons, men and women are irresponsible, and can't be relied on to stick around. One moment the Piazza is a crowd-scene, the next a desert, and this is where sculpture can play a major role by building permanent human interest into the scene. To such effect in the case of Borromini, 169, that the dead stone, by adding something to mere movement which we will call *action*, acquires more vitality than the living flesh it is about to attack. Both Loreto and Bergamo, 167, provide sculptural action, while the flesh, feathered or human, seldom rises above movement.

169

Inaction

Baroque sculpture is notorious for its anticipation of movie techniques, a fact which makes it as we have seen an important townscape aid. But similar results can be got by other means. No dead-stock could be deader than the sleeping dog, 171, yet its immobility impregnates the environment with movement, setting up tensions in the surrounding ether, a sort of electric field. A case of 'deadness' (or inaction)

intensifying livingness, the consequence no doubt of dynamic doggy associations in the mind of the beholder. But it doesn't have to be a dog. One expects and gets the same service from great (non-Baroque) sculpture—Marini's signalling horses for example, or Moore's downland dames.

171

Reaction

Car-worship of the extremist order provides, 170, another sort of sculpture, but of a kind one can only call an affront to the civil code of urban behaviour. Even those who are seduced by these charms would admit their incompatibility with any street outside Motopia. Difficult to account for the sense of outrage they arouse, unless for the reason already given, that the cabs 164, and oxen, 163, and even the scooters, 165, are chained to the town or its immediate environment, whilst the roadster is so clearly unchained as to constitute a challenge to the whole urban idea. Incivilia. Unwritten though clearly to be read on its sneering front glows the word gertcha.

Street Furniture

Movement, it is already clear, doesn't either in architecture or townscape demand motion in the literal sense. Nor the kind of parody provided by the Baroque architect. Robert Adam, a father of the classical revival, cultivated 'movement' in his buildings with passion. So did the medieval vault builders, and many of the objects here, the signpost shapes, 173, the curve of the curbs, 174, the Di Fiore script, 177, the Energol snakes, 175, the snakelike arms of the Bishop's chair, 178, the tread-marks in the mud, 168, are packed with movement. These are the bread-and-butter furnishings of the street, the objects of everyday service. In common with lamp-posts, bus-stops, hoardings, shop displays, parking meters, railings, pavings, fascias, street-names, neon, they determine eventually its character—so

inevitably that you would expect street furnishing to be an expertise practised by highly qualified specialists instead of what it is, an anarchy. The only person who takes the street seriously today is the townscaper for whom these objects are the vital instruments of his craft. Exciting always, sometimes surprising, like the text of the sign (in English) outside Lazise, 172.

178

179
180
181

182

Street Advertising

The alternative to anarchy doesn't have to be
dictatorship. There is still a sound jobbing-printer
tradition in Italy, 183, providing without benefit of
authority, civil or artistic, a robust service. The
poster, either stabile, 180, or mobile, 181,
qualifies in several ways as a friend of the street,
introducing movement as usual, colour always,
change of scale often, occasionally shock. Italics
or script are of course the conventional
typographical ways of working motion into print.
Giantism (the outsize word or eye), 179, is an
important falsifier of scale. Shock can occur when
some infamous hand, 182, shows up society as
composed of 'disruptive elements' instead of huge
conformities. Every street and wall of Siena was
recently plastered by this poster, a variation
upon the Guelf-Ghibelline theme, and a reminder
that poster-art is essentially contemporary, not to
say up-to-the-minute, the poor man's picture
gallery so-called. In England that phrase has been
responsible for the grave error of encouraging
bill-posting firms to provide picture frames for
hoardings in the mistaken belief that since a nice
picture needs a frame and someone once suggested
that posters are nice pictures, they, the posters,
will gain status by being framed. A psychological
error. Posters are ephemeral things and except on
theatres and cinemas should be shoved up in
accidental-looking places.

OCCASIONE DI BREVE DURATA
SOLO PER POCHI GIORNI
RIBASSI
dal 20 al 50 per cento
SSI  APPROFITTATE
r cento
SSI RIBASSI
 dal 20 l 50 per centa
SSI  APPROFITTATE
r cento

Display

Italy's advantage over other countries lies in the existence of civilized townscape habits many of which have survived industrialization and admass. It is still standard Italian practice to build every shopfront *within* the framework of the building, 185, (not as in England, botch it as an extra on to the façade) and then, if further display is required, pile the goods for sale outside. A practice which safeguards the homogeneity of the street and provides beguiling objects for the eye, birds, 186, nets, 187, night wear, 190. Not of course, sad though it is to lose the traditional butcher's shop, food— from the distant past one remembers other children besides Francis Bacon whose day was made by the diagrammatic half-carcass cleaving to the brass rail. Awnings, 188–9, or umbrellas, 184, can protect the display either from sun or rain, and in common with bed linen hung for airing from the bedroom window, 191, join utility and gaiety in marriage. Of the display possibilities of bed linen the Italians themselves are well aware. No festa passes without a great hanging-out of counterpanes, and any other bedroom-wear that happens to be around, a spontaneous act of bon-homie which makes flags and flag-wagging seem just a bit artificial.

188, 189, 190
191

192, 193

Levels of Feeling

Because many objects one normally deals with in
a town are utilitarian—signs, hydrants, fascias,
posters, window displays—it is a temptation to
treat street-furnishing as a commercial art, with
shallow values and trivial objectives. Fair enough,
so long as the thing remains at the elementary
level we operate to-day. Having lost the art of
making towns we are currently more than satisfied
to bring order out of chaos, tidy up a mess, clean
up commercial muddle. *Civilia*, however, offers
more positive promotions than mess-tidying. A
lion-head wall-fountain suffering the assault of the
bill-sticker, 192, can achieve a lyricism as strange
and forlorn as a Samuel Palmer: the sort of
wayside mural a child, passing to and from
school, would digest unconsciously and be enriched
by. Remembering always that the ultimate

purpose of town-making is to make more fruitful
the lives of *people*. At the other end of the
emotional scale, 193, murderous railings against
a sinister back-drop of nature-in-the-raw work
up an antithesis that turns the bowels to water.
Notice the detailing. The spikes of the fence had to
be sharp as swords to wring the cries of anguish
that now issue out of one's cringing psyche.
Borrowed merely from the pattern book of
Victorian tradition the railings would have
evoked no more than a swampy nostalgia. These
hurt. The same child passing to and from school
might pick up profitable hints here about
inhumanity—and nature—and learn to make
resolutions about his own.

194

Objects

Nostalgia

Swampy nostalgia in the last note suggests a
contempt no perceptive person feels. The surprising
thing is, how deep the impressions of those walks
from school at the age of five, six or seven, go.
The stationer at the corner, the lamp-post and
leaning laburnum, pond, cul-de-sac, railway
bridge, the train shovelling steam over its
shoulder (alas, not much longer). Once again,
affection doesn't necessarily entwine itself around
what is architecturally, visually or morally
'good'. Not much aesthetic virtue clings to the
letter box, 194, yet it is lovable and so is the
peeling wall. This brings us back to our first
axiom, that architecture and townscape, though
related, have little in common. Bad architecture
may make good townscape and bad townscape
come out of good architecture. To say it again,
townscape belongs to the stage rather than the
architect's drawing board, and its components,
once isolated as objects, are best assembled in
terms of 'theatre'.

Lazy Eye

Since, unlike the painter's hand, it doesn't select, the camera is an inefficient instrument when it comes to demonstrating a point. But so is the eye than which no organ is more easily tired—fairer perhaps to say more remorselessly over-worked. Its defence mechanism ranges from seeing everything (equivalent, that, to seeing nothing)— to the most irritating trick of all: selection-by-habit—which adds up to seeing nothing again.

Almost the only difficulties of the present investigation are the eye's bad habits, as one finds out when the camera stops concentrating on detail. The moment a general view, 195, turns up again it becomes a question of how many 'objects', in the sense used above, the eye does in fact still see. Or in the satisfaction of gaining a 'general impression' does it start at once to ignore the detail? This is where the re-alerting has to start. The shot below is in fact packed with dramatic

detail but before he can isolate it the lazy viewer
may have to cultivate the kind of reorientation
that occurs naturally when faced with the
negative instead of the print. In this one, 196,
arch, buttress, bollard, floor pattern, staircase
diagonal, leap out of the picture in precisely the
way one requires of a townscape image. The
problem is to train the eye to do automatically
what the negative achieves by surprise.

196

7

Earth

Not every citizen will become an addict of townscape but there are few who won't from time to time give a passing thought to the character of their environment. For such, Italian towns, *hill-*towns in particular, have a special message, since (as John C. Haskell* points out) they reveal in microcosm most of the basic urban ingredients found to a more complex and intense degree in larger towns and cities. *Hill-*towns because site conditions dictate the economical use of land and concise, compact and co-ordinated building forms.

With site conditions this study touches down, hits *earth* so to speak, first of the four elements under the heads of which what follows is to be carved up, for reasons which will become plain as we go on. Earth in this context covers any 'object' that lies, stands or rolls upon our base, the land, an *object* being that which, no matter how trivial, contributes to the artefact, *town*, and thus to the urban image, whether temple, road-surface, street corner, shop fascia or negligee exposed for sale. These are

*A 1955 Rome Scholar and Consultant to the Oxford Preservation Trust, writing in RIBA Journal, October 1962.

the hazards of the street in the sense that bunkers are the hazards of the golf-course. One might do worse indeed than treat the whole issue in golfing terms (tee, bunker, rough, fairway, green), an approach which puts the hazards in their right perspective as *teases* designed (in the case of golf) to make bearable the hard-labour of hitting a small ball with a long stick.

A good golf-course *looks* good, is a good tease one might say. To treat civic design as a tease-style art would no doubt be rather extravagant but it is not entirely out of order to represent the townscaper as a layer-out of visual 'obstacles' designed to stimulate the player of the urban game. As with golf it would be a falsification to say the hazards are there to make the game more difficult; they are there to make it more interesting, to which end the visual bunkering of the citizen is lovingly directed.

Not a new enterprise as it happens. The impulse to baffle in both meanings of the word might be called the first principle of Renaissance town-planning. Most of what follows deals with simple points but those who are moved to dismiss them as trivial might remember (in the mild words of Camillo Sitte) that they embody 'principles which in spite of platitudinous appearances are far from being observed today'.

Earth

Defensive Armour

The Mausoleum of Theodoric at Ravenna, 197, seen through its protective armour of iron and wire. As bad, this, as anything the Ministry of Works has done at Stonehenge, and not the only defaulter. As the reader will have noticed already (we hope) the fountain in the Via Vanucci at Perugia, 54, also carries a criminal record and has had to be put behind bars. The nature of the crime? Being too good for its company or, to put it the orthodox way, destructive youths. The wrong way. If a city's monuments are so fragile as to have to be guarded they aren't suitable for the street and should be shipped off to a museum. Repaired in the spirit of glum pedantry

198

199

native to all 'Restorers' the results at Perugia are so forlorn that little harm would come of rough handling by destructive youths. Youth can be destructive, granted, but no amount of vandalism can excuse the whole repudiation of Civilia which is implied by iron spikes or barbed-wire entanglements.

Constipation

Rome, 200, and Venice, 199, freer with their works of art, are a better model of Civilia than Perugia and Ravenna. The wickedness of destructive youths which seldom goes beyond crawling dangerously over a given monument doesn't necessarily do it wrong. The large bronze toes of the Colossus of Barletta (restored) have gained centuries of patina in a few years from the sandals and bare feet of hop-skip-and-jumping small-fry. Likewise the lion of S. Mark's whose battered beauty, 202, is more moving than the numb precision of the figures round Perugia's fountain. Rubbing shoulders, literally and metaphorically, with the town—and the townees —helps to make a monument come alive and, in return, paddling children and squatting women, 198, give it the importance it demands as a focal point.

Moral, don't lock up your fountains. Make them tough enough to stand up to destructive youths or pack them off to a museum. Putting Eros in a packing case on Boat Race night is a criticism of Eros, not undergrads. He needs to be climbed and ought to be all the better for it. So ought the undergrads. One of the functions of urban monuments is to provide that kind of exercise. And outlet. Towns can be constipated as well as people. The unconstipating of towns is a main preoccupation of the new school of town planners.

201

Earth

Toughies

The need for strength in urban sculpture, always
subconsciously present in the sculptor's mind,
has probably been responsible for the age-old
cult of the lion, savage at Viterbo, 203-4, fubsy at

Pitigliano, 201, rock-of-ages at Venice, 202, each tough enough however to look after himself in the battle of Incivilia. The two backs above can and do give—and through the centuries have given—rides to countless children without turning a hair, one the original shaggy dog, the other a map of life. Or perhaps eternity. Difficult to believe that two backs could be so expressive, or capable of such extremes of feeling, the extreme of doggy fortitude at Pitigliano, the extreme of arrogant vitality at Venice. Their fronts or sides can be seen in 205 and 207. Lions are made for this job but it is surprising how few animals are. A bear might be expected to make a good model but 208, also at Pitigliano, shows the difficulty the artist found in making a really chunky job.

Earth

203

204, 205

206, 207

Sissies

One alternative to packing away sissy sculpture in a museum is to place it like the bear, 208, at the top of his column out of reach of all but the chamber-pot crowners who are mostly mountaineers of a brand too professional to do damage on the climb. Another, which applies

208

particularly to statesmen in stone and bronze, is to expose the vital parts (luckily the head is a good round canon ball) and dispense with the impractical top hats at the end of spindly arms, the spindlier umbrellas, the buckling legs, the tottery feet. The benefactor of Baunei, 206, may not be great sculpture but the absence of spindly matters below the belt and the presence of half a mountain in their place, ensures a strong and handsome garden ornament. The wonderful

negro at Manfredonia with his swooping glissando of a back, 209, more voluted than the bear's, is well protected from destructive hands by the huge bunker that is his base. The old bruiser of S. Mark's, 207, a hangover from the previous note, and in fact out of place on this page, belongs to that other resounding back, 202.

210

211

212

213

Softies

Certain materials disintegrate in the open and these, like the great wooden horse in the Palazzo della Ragione at Padua or the wonderful equestrian statues of the Gonzagas at Sabbioneta, should be kept under cover. Here the need for protection against hooligans and the elements disappears and it is reasonable to go in for the sort of detail which would get rubbed off outside. The Gonzaga armour, for example. As Sabbioneta and its founder have already figured in a biggish way in this book, it may be of interest to record

the names and relationships of these equestrians. 210, 214, Ludovico Gonzaga 1414-1478, friend of Alberti and Second Marchese di Mantua. 211, Gian Francesco Gonzaga 1443-1496, youngest son of Ludovico and head of the Sabbioneta branch of the family. 212, Luigi Gonzaga 1500-1532, nicknamed Rodomonte on account of his fabulous strength and courage—grandson of Gian Francesco. 213, Vespasiano Gonzaga 1531-1591, son of Rodomonte and builder of Sabbioneta in the ten years between 1560-1570. His first wife, together with her lover, Vespasiano

personally despatched on a suspicion of infidelity. His second wife, Anne of Aragon, went the same way. For not doffing his hat when they met in the street he kicked his only son and heir (on whom he doted) so hard in the groin that he died. This was following a trepanning operation. The last ten years of his life were spent in building the two Sabbioneta churches as testaments to his remorse, for no one was more revolted by these acts than their author. The rage of life, he felt, was a disease, and when finally he turned his face to the wall his last words were 'I am cured'.

Unofficial Ornaments

Statues, fountains, obelisks, may be called the official ornaments of Civilia. In common with ornament elsewhere, when artlessly or inelegantly used they quickly become liabilities and even at their best only make frozen music of the conventional kind. More interesting because less publicized is the unofficial ornament, the costume jewellery, of the street, fashioned for use out of its functional requirements. Beyond the fountain in 215, looms *Fiumeter, affiliata all'INA* and *Campari,* and under the bowl of the shell snuggle street-users and shop-canopies, articles of a different order and scale yet creating in combination with the official monument the kind of rough poetry which appeared in the poster and lion-head on an earlier page. The poetry of multiple use: difficult to define, yet strongly

215

216
217

felt by sensitive citizens, arising as it does from
a perception of the variety of interlacing interests,
goals, purposes, patterns, passions, paths and
people. The Campari prospect doesn't exactly
please, yet as a ballet of the street it is moving
and something else as well, *strange*. Strangeness
is communicated again at Urbino, 216, where the
scene is cut up by wall-ends and taut double
wires into aedicules housing unrelated images—
back-yardscape, treescape, town-wall, the
wild—as quarterings to the frightening Personage
created out of the eagle's flank. Gay, garish,
pompous, pretty, beautiful, sublime, weird, brutal,
mad, monstrous—townscape, like landscape, can
ring the changes on the entire human dilemma.

143

top 218, 219; bottom 220, 221

Pile-up

A deeper dive into the unofficial topography of
the street reveals *objects,* in the sense used in the
introduction to this section, taking over their
full responsibilities. These have equal claims
with the official monuments to acceptance as
urban sculpture both in 221, the deliberate, and
218, the accidental form. Or in window-dressing
without the window. Display, but in another
sense to that already used. The pile-up (genteelism
and its ploys apart) is the secret of successful

shop décor and Italians are its supreme exponents.
Thus the bags at Florence market, 220 (notice
how easily they dominate the official sculpture),
thus the candles at Loreto, 219. The picture-
postcard technique, 222. Bookshops, chemists,
wine-merchants, grocers, greengrocers,
delicatessens—they all practise the pile-up with
consequences which make Italian shops, outside
or in, the most tempting in the world. The door-to-
door salesman, 223, is an unusual mobile in the
same tradition.

222, 223

225

224

Side-shows

Some of the most telling pile-ups are movable
ones, temporary in theory, permanent in practice.
Coffee-stalls, hot-dog stands, newspaper kiosks,
tobacconists and, in Paris of course, Gents. It
isn't for the town-planner to make the decision
which of these should go where, but his preference
will be for those which add texture to the scene.
Bouquet as well. Roman bananas have both and
any artist who is also a greengrocer is free to
create, 226, vegetable build-ups official
monuments can hardly hope to rival. In the
inorganic world magazines substitute for
vegetables, newsagents for greengrocers, and there
are artists in this trade too. No banana could ask
for a more suitable foil to its own convolutions
than the formal geometry of the printed page,
bunching too, but according to a formula of its
own. Behind the road builders, 224, where a

226

projection in the building line—called elsewhere
a wing or shoulder—introduces Padua's
glittering clock tower another news-stand, gay as
the clasp of a Quiz-Queen, 225, provides a perfectly
calculated urban ornament. Far from detracting
from the impact of the clock tower its
brilliance and intricacy echo the monument,
and double the vivacity of the scene as comparison
of one photograph with the other demonstrates.
224 also reveals roadwork as another
side-show of the movable kind, which, properly
impresario'd, can provide a pleasing don't-do-
it-yourself act for those not in the clutches of an
impatient car.

227

Repetition

The newsagent has the advantage of working to
a module in the form of a more or less standardized
unit, the Glossy, with a standardized content,
the female face, or form. In consequence he is able
to reap the benefits of repetition and many of
his trade are quick to grasp its possibilities.
The neat little kiosk at Perugia, 227, cheekily
burlesques the architectural detail of its austere
neighbour and so, by making Dead-Sea-tablets
(or their equivalents) of the rustications, tempts
the shopper to walk away with one of them
under his arm. No regional or geographical
limitations to this style, it could turn up in
East Sheen as easily as Padua or Perugia.
It seldom does. A pity, because as a style it is
intrinsically stylish.

Style

Style is sometimes confused with classiness (living in style). Wrongly. Living in style is classy but not stylish. Class is preoccupied with status symbols, style isn't—doesn't aim at 'good form' in the abstract, though in the concrete it aims at precisely that and nothing else. No one would be likely to suggest that *Upim's* is a genteel signature, but in a new and promising way, 228, it *is* stylish. *And* vulgar

228

in the Latin meaning. Something added to
popular art, popular style, a very different
article to ghastly good taste, being the product
of a get-up-and-go attitude to the modern thing.
Tubi, Di Fiore and *Cristani* though not quite so
good belong in the same genre, as also do
Lazise's umbrellas and chairs, 230 (almost
standard these days throughout the outside
cafés of Italy). Vulgar? If you say so. But stylish.
Popular style is not an entirely novel development,
as certain Victorian examples of the functional
tradition remind us, manhole covers, for one.
Viterbo, 229, only wants to hang on a wall to be
received as great art, and from the same
tradition a trickle of congenial things-of-use in
the shape of pots and pans still fill a hundred
piazzas on Market Day. Compare the lordly

229

231

232, 233, 234

simplicity of this kitchen-ware, 231, with the tortured art-work, 233-5-6-7-8 that swarms around the curio and trinket shops along the *route touristique*. These little horrors, symptoms of chara-pox, and spreading with the ugly celerity of that fell disease, have already made intolerable once lovely places like Assisi, San Marino and Monte S. Angelo. To the list of stylish articles whose watchword is fitness to purpose it would be nice to add traffic signs, but though the tide of highway-code taste is rising (and despite what is said on the next page) there is still, 234, plenty of room for improvement. With a few exceptions like P for Parking our international traffic symbols are infantile or badly presented and sorely in need of re-styling.

Public Style

We now come to a still more hopeful phenomenon, public style, the achievement of Local, County or Government Departments, indicating an understanding by Authority of what style is and does, starting with the development of a visual highway code founded on what *The Architectural Review* has called the nautical tradition. Essential features, simplicity, ecomony, legibility, definition, with, understandably, more and more reliance on nautical black and white. A clear expression of function. Formed in those austere yet evocative characters, Baunei, 239,

becomes a place for the imagination to toy with, an Italian Yarrow Unvisited. The cat's-eyes are hardly less distinguished. High spot in this authoritarian climb out of barbarism is perhaps the lamp standard. In the post-war years the use of metal vapour lighting (mercury sodium or mercury fluorescent) has created a visual revolution on the street, in England, at the hands of the Ministry of Transport, an almost uniformly bloody one. Outrage in concrete is giving ground at last to burly steel monuments some of them not bad monuments as monuments go, but we don't want monuments, we want lamp standards—sleek articles that do their job with grace and a maximum of modesty. Everywhere but in England the problem is well understood and for the last ten years a single type, 240, as elegant as it is practical, has been gradually populating Europe. Notice how

239

Earth

240
241

tactfully it genuflects before the oldie worldie
while remaining an active adherent of the
functional aesthetic as projected by the railings
or their shadows, 241. Superb detailing, style at
its best and most public. If you are Anglo-Saxon
consider what visual disasters would have been
avoided in British streets and motorways had the
Ministry of Transport adopted this gilded shape
from the beginning and made certain it was
universally used.

242, 243

Earth

244

Class

After style, class. Street furniture should consist of more than lamposts and railings, the bare bones, these, of the town. Pure architecture is a bore to everyone but pure architects. Hence people on the wrong side of the tracks like to hang out flags in the form of washing, 244, though the day is coming, as we have seen, when sheets, towels, shirts, may no longer decorate either alley or back-garden. A serious thought. Where class forbids such displays, other forms of furnishing—ironwork, trellis, paint and planting —take up the running. 242 and 243 are two of a kind from the same town, Alassio. One remains unashamedly prole, the other aspires to bourgeois status by various means: more intricacy, more

ironwork, creepers, pot plants, paint, a well-heeled air of smugness, all those little fripperies which make it a class product. Result, transformation, from the *Mediterranean vernacular* to the *Riviera style*, idiom of the cushioned classes everywhere, international, that is, and just as much at home in Cheltenham as on the Cote d'Azur. Not stuck-up either, living in close harmony with its non-white-collar neighbour, a thing to note. Middle-class blight has been responsible for covering so many million acres of Europe with charlatanry that we tend to identify the bourgeois with the bogus when in fact bourgeois culture has merely been going through a bad patch induced by the general madness of the industrial revolution.

249

Propriety

As we have seen (and as Baroque architecture
would demonstrate if we hadn't) economy of means,
though often promoting it, isn't synonymous
with style whatever literary purists may say. Nor
—whatever the British may think—is reticence.
It is difficult on the other hand to conceive a
stylish object that lacks propriety—propriety as
opposed to fitness; fitness transferred to the
emotional plane. Strangely, in a nation whose
main characteristics are supposed to be passion
and impulse, it is their sense of fitness, meaning
feeling for propriety, that astonishes the
foreigner in his dealings with Italians as
townscapers. Reserve where required, display
where apt. Lacking the building or planning
regulations which have tried and manifestly
failed to regulate the pattern of development of
the industrial nations, the Italians have somehow
achieved many of their goals. Hardly a town but
has a working by-pass. And access to the country.
No suburban sprawl. From the north to the south
buildings come down to the ground and shops are
found inside them instead of tacked by shop-

fitters onto the façade. Hence their wonderfully homogeneous character, which seems to have side-stepped a whole cycle of vulgar outrage and abuse. Homogeneity is not, of course, the same thing as monotony, any more than display necessarily acts as a stimulus—by commercial display English towns, once full of character, have been reduced to a dead-level of dullness in which one enormous chain-store fascia after another, Timothy White, International, Sainsbury, Marks & Spencer, Woolworth, Odeon (the banks are a little better), bludgeons the High Street into insensibility. Worse, impersonality. To-day the sole difference between one High Street and another lies in the order of appearance of the chain-gang. Far too late to be any use, signs of grace are now appearing in these relentless salesmen, but you only have to read the words U P I M, 228, to see what a chasm in *sense of propriety* as well as style separates Italian from English or American chain-store psychology. In Italy, as we have said already, the shop, 185, stays inside the building though the merchandise may come out. Again, though Italian films occupy a high position as popular art, the Italian cinema doesn't try to monopolize or dominate the street. In city after city, 245-6-7-8-9, you find the cinema occupying not a back street but a back seat, often an old façade. Where conditions call for a new building, though architecturally it may be as squalid as its English opposite number, the siting is so arranged—at Foligno through an archway in the Cassia 250-1—as not to interfere with the town's established character. Repeat, *established* character. In new towns the issues are different. With galloping prosperity and a general souping-up of the rat-race good principles may totter but one hopes that propriety—the Italian sense of fitness—will still prevail. New techniques of publicity may help. Neon for one, which has played a significant part in cleaning up street advertising. By day discreetly calligraphic, it adds by night a new dimension to the metropolitan scene.

250
251

Display

Display to-day is generally (and rightly) regarded as something to be stuck onto rather than built into our architecture. Like flags. But it is worth remembering that this is a matter of fashion rather than principle. Nothing in the history of self-advertisement has surpassed the feats of the Palazzo builders whose sham castles will still be stamping the names Pitti, Strossi, Medici, upon history long after Woolworth and Burton have gone into limbo. No salesmanship in the accepted sense, no fascia boards, no plugging of slogans, no buying of space. The exhibitionism lies in the architecture itself, in the case of Pitti 254-5-6, the mere size of the stones, Cyclopean, unforgettable, Etruscan. Display in kind; more effective than drapes when done with genius; though the standard Italian way of clothing building sites, 253, shows how effective drapery could be were it ever architecturally employed. This impulse, when it comes, is generally converted into paint and the small-scale punch (like the painted diaper in 252) can be as full of punch in its own way as the outsize rustication.

Earth

253

257

Articulation

There is a point at which architectural display
builds up to storm proportions to be
described later as violence, and another at which
the pressure moderates from mummery (the
rustications) to the (not necessarily functional)
expression of function. Articulation, so
called, the test of which lies in the performer's
capacity to make detail integral. Without moving
from the foot-super of pavement he occupies at the
moment, let any interested person cast his eyes
down to the pavement's junction with the base of
the adjacent building, a crucial architectural test
many points of junction fail to pass. The example
chosen here, 257, has met with approval from one
citizen at least using criteria which aren't perhaps
ours, but if we eye his couch, from an angle which

164

isn't his, it isn't difficult to admire the
masterly way in which the transition is
achieved from pavement to base and base to
building. First a kerb, a sort of feed-line formed
of the stuff of the Palazzo not the pavement, then
the bolection moulding, then the continuous
stone tie-beam, refusing to break continuity even
when challenged by the basement windows whose
heads, created by a switch in materials, complete
the first term of the base. The second is
articulated by the huge consoles which descend
like grappling irons within a few feet of the floor
ready to dig in their hooks should the Palazzo
start to take off. Not merely strong, exciting, a
favourite Italian formula which loses nothing by
repetition and illustrates the episodic nature of
close-range architecture when seen as townscape:
the right way (for all but architects) to see it.

Violence

A recurring Italian urge revolves around the
need for stairs in open spaces, fetish, perhaps, of
a hill-top people. Utility is clearly not the first
consideration, the exploration of space is, and
the articulating of it by formal means. Here
we come up against this strange capacity
for communicating violence, Bernini-wise, to
what is, after all, only a tread and riser—
passionate builders of stairs have somehow

succeeded in becoming builders of passionate stairs. Passionate stairscape is much in evidence in a hundred places and draws its strength from the determination to let the riser do its own business with a minimum of tarting up. At Todi, 258, not even a handrail. At Arezzo, 261, and elsewhere, 260, 262-6, no articulation of any sort. Another example of Italian fundamentalism, still (as the passionate *modern* staircase in 259 demonstrates) very much alive.

259 260 261

267
268

Earth

Changes of Level

Stairs, 267, permit vertical exploration of space. To
see another member of your species operating far
above or below you violates the flat-earth theory
and as such is 'romantic'. Romantic is the term
the guide books use for staircase towns (Campo-
basso, Clovelly), meaning exciting but mad. The
flat-earth alternative is of course the prairie,
hence prairie planning, but there is an obvious
half-way house, the hill, despised and rejected of
all modern town-planners before Cumbernauld, but
for the townscaper one of his prime requirements.
It doesn't have to be 1 in 4 like 269 and 270. Small
changes of level lend themselves to large effects
and can be exaggerated by tricks such as that at
Bergamo, 268, where a common wall by dividing
opposite gradients doubles the impact of each.

271

272
273

Floor Pattern

With floor pattern we come down literally to
earth where it would be wise to stay long enough
to consider how vital it is to find modern
equivalents of the materials which have made
floors interesting, 274, throughout the centuries.
Because stone paving, 273, setts, 272, and cobbles
271, no longer meet all requirements we tend to
accept tarmac as the only practical means of
covering heavily used pieces of the world. Thus
is Civilia reduced to frustration at its base, the
floor, since the laying of endless acres of macadam
or asphalt is calculated to defeat the purposes of
townscape before they ever get started. The floor
is a large area and unless it is well articulated
it becomes, like any other large empty slab of

274

earth, a desert, or dustbowl. How careful our
predecessors were to create floor-pattern 275, 278-9,
280-1, show, and, having far more floor to pattern
and far greater opportunities in terms of materials
and techniques for ringing the changes, it is
surely lazy and feckless of modern road makers

275, 276

to reduce their routines to one. Concrete itself
provides variations and firms like Pirelli have
already produced stylish solutions in rubber, some
of which grace the surrounds of the Pirelli building
in Milan, others Florentine pavements, others, 276,
the floor of Rome station. There should in fact be
as much variety in floor surface as in scale and
purpose of streets and Alberti has already
reminded us how many varieties of streets there
are or ought to be. Fitness for purpose suggests
that each floor demands its own specific type of
articulation, macadam for the arterial street,
something very different for the alley. The
borough engineer's little habit of stripping the
pedestrian network of cobbles, paving, bricks,
and replacing them with universal tar is an
outrage which must be discontinued. Consider
the visual consequences of asphalting 274, 278, 279,
280, 281. The children in 280 remind us of something
else as well, how much of liberty of action can be
restored to human beings by a healthy pedestrian
network.

277

273

Earth

280, 281

Covering the Floor

One way to work pattern into a dustbowl is to sow
it with objects, 282. Nice on market day when the
objects themselves are attractive or stimulating,
not so nice when their associations are hostile to
those of the space they fill. Cars, for example. The
Piazza Ducale at Mantua must be one of the largest
open spaces in Europe. Its floor pattern is ancient,
and though adequate to any rather smaller area,
would hardly stand up to this enormous gap, 284,

283

282

were support not forthcoming from the side-lines
in the shape of towers, domes, theatres and temples
at heights which guarantee a genuine sense of
enclosure. A practical demonstration of Sitte's
axiom that the maximum dimension of a square
ought not to exceed twice the height of the
principal buildings bounding it. However, at most
operative times the question either of area or
floor-pattern doesn't arise, since, except in the very
early morning when this picture was taken, neither
the Piazza Ducale's floor nor its spatial
attributes are candidates for serious discussion.
To discover why, please turn to the next page,
which shows the same scene four hours later.

Earth

288, 289
290

The Shape of things to come

Jane Jacobs describes* how in American cities
Corbusier-style town planning, far from creating
arboreal amenities in the shape of open space
between blocks, has merely encouraged a vaster
in-fill of greater car-parks. One can see the same
process beginning on the L.C.C. estate at
Roehampton and Europe in general is rapidly
approaching the sort of apotheosis attained
already at Mantua. These shots, 285-6-7-8-9-
290, are taken from the opposite end to that on
the previous page and show the mid-morning
view left, right and centre of the Cathedral which
is the giant-pilastered building in the background.
Anyone who prefers his scenery served up on a
thick lining of car-roofs or conceives Tourism in
terms of a continental progress from one capital P
to another should put the Piazza Ducale on his
itinerary. Nowhere else will he have it so good.
*In 'The Death and Life of Great American Cities', Jonathan Cape.

Parking

It is the standing car which is the menace of our
age. If all cars kept moving there would hardly
be a traffic problem. But then cars themselves
would be redundant. They have the edge on other
forms of transport—aircraft for example—
precisely because they act as door-to-door
salesmen. And then sleep on the front step. Out
of all the foreground-to-middle-distance cars
shown in 292 only five are moving. This is not the
place to discuss off-street parking but insofar
as parking has to be tolerated at all it is better
policy to park on the streets, dedicated as they
are to congestion anyway, than on the piazzas
built to relieve it. Possible exceptions to this rule
are very high, narrow, gloomy, enclosures like
the Piazza of the Uffizi, 293, which seems to be
humanised (or unmannerised) by the presence of
charas; and spaces so enormous that they cease
to act as lungs and become leaks. Leaks are the
equivalent of blitzed areas, gaps in Civilia. The
Place de la Concorde is one, the Piazza del
Popolo, 291, another, an area civically speaking
so vast that though it is also splendid there is a
case to be made for peopling it with car-bodies
kept in lines of mathematical precision and so
restoring the pattern forefeited by sheer size. In
contrast with the Piazza Ducale at Mantua
there is still plenty of open space here
even when the cars have done their worst.

291, 292, opposite page, 293

Earth

294

295
296
297

Secretion

The ideal is of course secretion, well understood at
Lazise where the main car-park, tucked away
behind the quays and the caravan camp, is a model
of invisibility. Although sited on the waterfront,
walls and planting, 295, disguise it from the
promenader except when passing, 294, the main
gates. At the same time the caravanners share all
the pleasures of the lido. By the exercise of a little
ingenuity it is surprising what a lot *can* be tucked
away. The weeping willow, 296, an admirable piece
of stage-scenery, does another valuable job in
acting, 297, as a bicycle shed. Not the ideal things
to find under a weeping willow, a car and a pile of
bikes, but a good deal better than having them
out in the open.

Official Face

The first of the three faces of Italy mentioned in
the introduction to this book (p. 16) was called
the official face. This has to be approached with
the sort of reserve the cynic keeps for glorious-
England-style advertising by petrol companies
whose ultimate interest lies in destroying by more
passionate motoring the heritage they celebrate.
In the same spirit the local authority
at Viterbo is at this moment destroying the

299
300
301

Lake of Bolsena by handcuffing it to a motorway.
Almost unbelievable, but once false principles
get a hold they take a lot of breaking. The face
presented by official photography is of the same
brand. An official face-saver operating on Todi
Cathedral would show a great building approached
by an austere flight of steps rising out of shadows
arranged where they will do most good, 298, a
simple way of reassuring addicts of Civilia
all's well with the world when in fact a more
honest photographer would record (and did) a
very different picture of the scene. Like Mantua,
the main square at Todi, 300, is at most operative
times of the day in full capitulation to the usual
highly licensed army-of-occupation. 301 shows
the same scene looking the other way.

Pious Parking

The use of the Cathedral Square as a car-park raises an issue technically connected with parking but otherwise important because of the clash of secular and sacred interests. The street is a free-for-all and there's no call to keep God out of it any more than the Devil. Still, many people feel that the more tragic or majestic symbols of the religious experience lose something if exposed to petrol fumes and girdle ads. The ban seems to apply to figures like the Pieta, 303, rather than symbols like the cross, 302, which in the context of the street would lose rather than gain religious significance by the addition of the figure of Christ. Gibberd* shows how a bit of paving and a cross is able to create (at Ciboure) a religious island in the profane scene, and a moving example of the same thing exists at Lazise where a stone cross, unfenced and unprotected, achieves a note of solemnity which

* 'Town Design', Architectural Press, 4th Edition 1962.

302
303

304   305

survives the rat-race atmosphere of the quays.
No railing off, no floor pattern, no planting. The
first photograph taken ten years ago, 304, shows
the powerful effect of this economy, the second,
305, taken recently, the use to which the space is
currently put. Failing an order not to, drivers
use it for what comes naturally, even those who
should know better; the author of this work for
instance, whose car occupies more space in the
picture than anyone else's. It spent a week there,
sometimes alone, more often in company, for one
car will attract others as honey attracts bees.
No excuse. A large car-park exists a few
revolutions further on. The moral? Drivers must
be discouraged by law from regarding every
available open space as the equivalent of a
yacht basin. Authority currently turns nasty
only when street circulation is threatened.

308

The Writing on the Floor

The traffic problem arises from the very human
desire to enjoy the benefits of an amenity without
paying for it. Cars need large dance floors to
waltz about on and larger side-lines for sitting it
out, and dance-floors cost money and take up
room. The first thing to remember is that all
solutions are wrong that sacrifice a town to its
traffic problem. A town is a place to live in—
better to sacrifice the traffic than the town.
However, the planner aims to sacrifice neither,
and for him certain rules need to be established.
If the first is, Don't sacrifice the town, the second
is, Don't treat the existing traffic problem as
chronic—Don't make the mistake of thinking
to-day's problem will be tomorrow's. At the
current rate of progress all our present plans will
be out of date in ten years and means of transport
may themselves have changed, a thought which
immediately inspires another Don't—Don't make
long-term decisions about a problem that calls
for short-term, opportunist, experimental
solutions. A matter of principle, this, well
illustrated by the contrast of method in the
Piazza Signoria at Florence and London's
Parliament Square, where Grey Wornum was
made to produce at colossal expense a *permanent*
break-up of the floor area in the interest of a
traffic flow which will certainly have to be
modified before the stones have weathered. Italian
traffic planners keep a better sense of proportion,
particularly about the temporary nature of the
problem. Rather than tamper with the floor itself
—an act that would commit them to the
permanent solution, they write on it, 306, a
sensible device which leaves an historic open
space unmodified by fiddlededee and allows the
planner to think again when new circumstances
arise. As they will. When they do, nothing is
simpler than to rub out the old drawing and make
a new one.

309

193

310

Floor writing has the enormous townscape attribute of not messing up the scene. Or changing it, except by adding pattern where pattern is badly wanted, on the floor. The zebra's horizontals in 310 complement the verticals of the colonnade (of S. Peter's) and while doing the practical job of making going-to-church slightly less murderous actually heighten the impact of the peristyle. A good example of the virtues of the nautical tradition, a language of symbols combining boldness with elegance and fitness. Rome now possesses some highly dynamic floor-writing, all of it wordless but in intention as clear as a foghorn. No car must cross the striped squid, 311, nailed there to make a bad crossing safe (and incidentally articulating a desert of tarmac—idiot English bureaucratic reaction: What happens in snow?). And on a main artery, 312, could any symbols hold more menace than these flighting arrows whose speed is doubled by opposition, as in moving staircases going opposite ways. The chap in the background who has certainly got the message is belting across a totally empty street in terror of his life. Another example, perhaps, of the Italian tradition of violence which reappears again in the fantastic length of the zebras spanning the Piazza Signoria, 308, 309, or the passionate floor-writing at Iseo, 313, 314. Such is the violence here that even Cinzano seems to have capitulated to the nautical style. Only a beginning, this. Nautical-style floor-writing for which tarmac

311 312

makes a good though not the only possible blackboard, 306, 307, is certain to develop in a big way in the next years, ousting a wilderness of bad traffic signposts and signals and ranging in character from surrealist shocks on the Rieti-Rome road, 315—the moon in the middle is formed of white shingle—to the functional elegance of a sports arena or tennis court, 308. For cars, as for balls, the double line means out-of-court, so most of the Piazza Signoria is still pedestrian. Notice how prettily lines alternate with studs, a combination which gives 309's zebra a more polished finish than 308's.

315, 316

Pedestrian Network

Of all the traffic signs the one above, 316, is the most significant—and most familiar. It is a reflection on the enormous difference between one country and another in general approach to the traffic problem that in England this sign, though familiar, is hardly used. Not used at all in its peripatetic Italian capacity as a temporary prohibition mounted on a movable base. It means *Closed to All Vehicles*, not *No Entry*. There is a difference and the notice below gives times when transit is allowed for the unloading of freight. One chap in 317 is obeying, the other breaking, though only just, the law by being astride his bike on this Ravenna street. At Ascoli Piceno the whole town square, 318, is out of bounds day and night to vehicles (except those that can be walked) though often fully occupied by market stalls. Almost empty when the market isn't operating it becomes glamorous soon after the siesta when the greatest of all Italian urban institutions, the *Passeggiata*, fills the void with a mass of handsome faces and

317

319

320

321

318

starling noises. In every town in the country this promenade of the citizenry takes place in the cool of the evening, starting about 6.0 p.m., 319, rising to a crescendo at 7.0, 320, and gradually falling off after 8.0, 321, with, by custom, strict limits to the area covered and much retracing of steps. To counter the barometric argument (it-couldn't-happen-here) these shots were taken in late September when (as pullovers and jackets show) the weather is little different from ours. In fact the *Passeggiata* takes place in many an English high

street and main road but remains unofficial
because unauthorized because unacknowledged by
Authority, hence unaided by the police. In Rye
Lane, Peckham, for instance, where all bus drivers
develop ulcers because the pedestrians have
captured the roadway. Rather a barren victory since
the chance of a bus treading on your heels is
enough to take the spice out of the achievement.
In the North the practice is even more widespread,
so why not do what the Italians do, deny the

323

promenade to vehicular traffic at certain crucial times of the day? At Vicenza this denial isn't required since Palladio doubled the pedestrian promenade with the main street to the great advantage of all, including the farmers, 322, who in this shot make an unconventional foreground to a monument familiar to every architectural student, the Palazzo del Consiglio. But in many places, Perugia for one, come seven in the evening, the Corso Vanucci, the city's Piccadilly, is roped off,

323, for pedestrian promenade whether the motor traffic likes it or not. It doesn't. An unbalanced town, Perugia has a maw that swallows traffic at one end without the ability to spew it out at the other so that when Vanucci is sealed cars can more or less abandon hope. Who cares? Certainly not the citizens. How great the need to perambulate is, is illustrated in 323, taken this time in October. Verona has gone one better and permanently sealed off, for pedestrian use only, what amounts to its own Regent Street, the Via Mazzini, 324, an act of courage which has paid dividends by imposing a traffic cartwheel and so creating a city-sized roundabout with Mazzini, Bra and Erbe as rather a large hub. Where transverse traffic cuts across Mazzini internal combustion has to give way to slacks and skirts, with results anyone familiar with the Italian character could foresee. The uncomic strip on the right tells the story, starting

with an object lesson in floor layout, 326, which must be almost unique in showing the pedestrian pattern taking precedence of the vehicular (stone flags interrupting tarmac). This means that the car in 327 is forced to stop to let the privileged classes pass, which, knowing Italians, means that that car is going to be lucky not to stay there for the rest of the day. The white car in 328, which came up later, saw a gap and charged through but 329 shows the

324

black one still caught in the pedestrian network.
The shot, of course, is looking up the vehicular street
with the pedestrian way crossing at right angles, and
though one is sorry for the black-car driver, it is
nice to celebrate for once an example of pedestrian
top-doggery in a case where the rivals meet in a
head-on clash. On the larger issues the Italian
traffic problem, more insoluble than ours on
account of the terrain, has, perhaps for that reason,
been attacked with more resolution. Segregation,
by-passes, under- and over-passes are all used as a
matter of course. Rome has numerous disguised
clover-leafs, a majority of one-way streets, a major
tunnel through the centre of the town and underpasses to all the bridges over the Tiber. Perugia's
tunnel underpasses the entire city. The Flaminia
at Spoleto is at this moment being taken through
the mountain not to avoid the town which it
already by-passes but to shorten the by-pass. In
Bologna, a city a hundred times smaller than
London, a pedestrian complex with shops and
services rabbit-warrens the entire area of the
Centro, about a quarter mile square. By comparison
the dives at Piccadilly Circus and Hyde Park
Corner seem a bit of a joke. So do our motorways
when compared with the thousand miles of the
Strada del Sole, bridging valleys, drilling
mountains. Through all these major works of
engineering, however, one Italian principle remains
constant, to solve the traffic problem if it can be
done, but never, never, never, sacrifice the town.

325

326
327
328
329

Car versus Cafe

If Perugia is redoubtable and Verona courageous Spoleto is positively heroic. Despite by-pass and under-pass the town's traffic problem is still practically insoluble and comes to a head, or rather bottle-neck, at the top of the hill in the

Piazza della Libertà and Via Salare Vecchia, 330, through which every single piece of through-traffic has to go. There wouldn't anyway be room for the cars were the entire pavement area to be sacrificed but far from adopting the 'normal' traffic-engineer's attitude—get the traffic through

331, 332

333

and damn the consequences—the local authority
has taken precisely the opposite view, damned the
consequences to the traffic and, in a street already
far too narrow for its pay-load, laid down duck-
boards, 330, to make the pavement wide enough for
cafe-society. A museum example of the tiny margin
between total urban defeat and total urban victory.
The waiters, 331, are on the duck-boards or, 332,
crossing the street to the bar on the other side
regardless of the queue of cars from which the
café-tables are protected by the usual line of
pot-plants. Transformation from motorway to
hurly-burly.

Hurly-Burly

The thing suggested by the title is relative. In a
village square, 335, two cars and a gang of children
make a crowd. In the city you need a lot going
on to get the authentic sense of bustle. Despite
the chi-chi cafe umbrellas on the front at Iseo, 336,
there still seems a good deal too much tarmac,
until market day, 337, makes the whole thing right.
One solution is the permanent market, precisely
what Florence has, complete with its own
permanent pavilion, in the Mercato Vecchio, 333,
a top-ranking piece of townscape made brilliant by
the vistas through the arcades. Similar vistas on
all four sides keep the space fluid and congruous
with the open street, so preventing any suggestion
that the building is *a building*.

Remoteness

Genuine remoteness is for the bloody-minded.
Most of us get embarrassed alone on mountain
tops faced by what Dostoevsky called the silence
of the universe. Moral remoteness, however, is a
luxury, a perquisite only a highly integrated
society can provide. The victory over promiscuity;
the feeling that although you may be within a few
yards of others you are sequestered, not trampled
into the ground by the herd. Difficult to achieve
in a city, yet done with success again and again,
notably in university towns. Notably too in Rome,
where low-level quays, 334, are gradually replacing
the mud along the Tiber. Down on the quays one

has a sense of isolation, of being withdrawn a
hundred miles from the city. The traffic pouring
over the bridges seems to belong to another
dispensation and doesn't destroy the illusion,
enhances it. In a way remoteness is at its most
pregnant within spitting distance of the hurly-
burly. Coventry City Centre is an English example,
where the roof car-parks provide a delightful sense
of isolation.

Outrage

When people or markets or cafe tables can't provide it the traditional cure for a dead patch in the town is a monument, sometimes by this race of extremists carried to extremes with the springing of a very canny townscape trick which consists in forcing a quart-size monument into a pint-size Piazza. Museum example, the Trevi fountain, 338, depending for its effect, like a poster, on outrage to the conventional urban scale. More violence. Biggest of all these sculptures, occupying the greatest available space in the smallest possible enclosure, is the Florentine dirigible known as the Duomo, 91. From none of the many approaches to it can this monument be really *seen*, a fact which fills the artless planner with despair while giving the sophisticate much quiet satisfaction.

338

339
340

Theatre

Most towns have to be satisfied with a more
modest line in sculptures than Florence Cathedral
and here an admirable habit survives of using the
monument to aid the build-up of the stage-set
rather than horsing around with axes and centres.
Iseo Market, 337, leads to the town square, 339, 340,
another example, the square, of townscape's
independence of capital-A Art. The architecture is
nice but undistinguished and the statue a joke, but
what a good bit of theatre the whole thing is, and
how admirably the joke-statue half bunkers the
entering street.

Waxworks

The Piazza at Forli, on the other hand, 341, is
five-star stuff with monumental trees, palatial
palaces and no less than six *tours de force* in the
persons of the church's circular brick columns—
complete with entasis. Super, all of it, yet in
townscape terms the ensemble, though much
presuming, never comes alive, nor can one conceive
it doing so even with a crowd-scene thrown in.
Waxworks, not theatre.

Multiple Use

If what has just been said is thought to insinuate that architecture and townscape are incompatible, turn to the Piazza Erbe at Verona where great architecture and sculpture mix with the populace in what is probably Europe's most successful example of multiple use. Traffic arrangements included. The confinement of vehicles, 342, to three sides of the square permits a pedestrian overflow, 346, throughout the whole area occupied by the market, with, in so far as the cafes allow it, penetration from the fourth side. An ideal arrangement. The market buffers the cafes from the traffic and the citizen has a delightful sense of being lost in the crowd—noise animated; scents (of flowers and greengroceries) delectable; the scene (from a cafe table) worthy of an oriental bazaar. Open space used as it should be to heighten the urban congestion and so multiply social contacts.

Enclosure

Open space is, of course, a misnomer. There should be nothing open about the right kind of urban lung. Like the Piazza Erbe, it should be another essay in enclosure, and is best thought of as an open-air room in the tradition of the Piazzetta at Venice, called by Napoleon *le plus beau salon de l'Europe*. Frederick Gibberd (in *Town Design**) resurrects Winifried Leonhardt's 'Space-bodies' from *Bauen* where she makes, on the *repousse* principle, space of the buildings surrounding a given square, and buildings of the spaces they enclose, thus substituting the idea of *roominess* or spatial volume for *open* space. He does so to make Sitte's point that floor area and spatial volume are not equivalents, or, rather, that the *effect* of spatial volume isn't dependent on the *amount* of floor area—the great and famous open squares—Erbe again—are mostly much smaller

* London: The Architectural Press.

342

than they appear. Indeed, after a certain point an
inverse ratio begins to operate—the greater the
floor area the less the sense of spatial volume, a
lesson never learnt by Beaux Arts architects. His
conclusion, that after excessive floor area street
openings are the greatest threat to spatial volume,
is shared by most planners, and leads him to
examine various alternatives starting with 343,
where the streets meet at right-angles on the
corners of the square. Sitte condemned this
arrangement as making breaches in the space-
body (an over-generalization, as we shall see
later), maintaining that earlier planners in order
to get overlapping façades, 344, avoided where
possible more than one street entering a corner,
They preferred 345, in which every entrance
into the enclosure is baffled by a building:
a practice so common that Sitte concluded it
must have been a principle, conscious or
unconscious, of traditional city planning. Be that

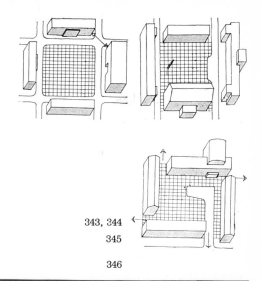

343, 344

345

346

as it may, 345 is the cue for the entrance of the
T-trap, a character which plays, as we have
seen, a significant role in Cinquecento townscape,
indeed at one stage practically steals the show.
Other variations are possible but none are more
than rules-of-thumb. The Piazza Garibaldi at
Sabbioneta flouts them all, starting with 343,
and gets away with it by means already
described (not to confound Sitte or Gibberd but
as a demonstration of the guile by
which a good townscaper can overcome his
liabilities) consisting in this case of no less than
eight entering streets, four of them at the two
western corners. The fact is, in matters of
townscape diagrams fail and the artist is
forced back on the eye or, failing that, its
stand-in, the camera. The eye, as we have
discovered already, is all the Italians have ever
bothered about, on the principle that what does
not offend that organ cannot outrage the mind.
Thus re-affirming the implicit Italian philosophy,
that rules and rulers and compasses and dividers
should be in the heart of the beholder and not the
hand of the artist. Townscape is by the same
token a matter of hunches rather than a system
of principles. Such hunches may not always be
fully self-conscious but they are the fruit of a
philosophy of life just the same.

349

Leaks

And a philosophy of town. One that is concerned
now with substituting the idea of enclosure for
open space. And thus of stopping leaks, a tactic
considered in greater detail earlier apropos the
street. Here two piazza examples are given to show
how far from rule-of-thumb the business is. One at
Orvieto, orthodox, the other, at Tarquinia, very
much the opposite. The Orvieto shot, 348, taken
from the Cathedral steps, has its sights trained
on the corner of the Piazza where the main
street enters under the tower. But does it? If so,
where? One can't tell. Repeat, *main* street, yet the
feeling of enclosure is absolute. One is not even
conscious of the existence of an entry or exit. The
other at Tarquinia, 347, presents on the face of it
just the opposite story. It is quite a common
practice in towns of this sort to prove the rule by
an exception. After many enclosures, suddenly
a street straight and ultra-wide. This act of
rebellion the builders of Tarquinia have
committed in the town square with a ploy
reminiscent of the fourth-wall omission beloved of

Baroque planners. The wide promenade that
breaks away up the hill from the Piazza is more
than a leak, it is a gap. However, by extending a
shoulder of building to act as a proscenium arch
they have succeeded in transforming the whole
scene. Suddenly the gap becomes a stage-set with
stage-scenery—the trees—and as the illusion
grows the gap diminishes until there is no gap,
no leak, nothing but impatience for the play to
begin. Anticipation—the mood of the playgoer
immediately preceding the rise of the curtain—
in this case the urge to breast the hill and get
an eyeful of whatever is cooking over the
horizon—has created a barrier to the negative
idea and with that barrier filled the gap. For
once the photograph represents rather well the
part played by the sky in this action. Instead of
roaring in to blow open the town it drops behind

350   351

the stage to make a back-cloth, and so a curtain, and so (though itself the recognized source of leakage) an unwilling agent of fresh enclosure. Notice the brilliant use of poster-banners.
By way of compensation for all this open air the fountain, 350, is employed in making cosy corners for those who need them.

Baffles

In the proscenium arch at Tarquinia and the shoulder introducing it, we make contact with a familiar motif, discussed earlier (in the section on *the street*) under the title *Wings*, a simple baffle for widening, diminishing, segregating or cordoning off an open space. At Bergamo, 351, it is used to carve a little enclave out of the street itself, thus forming the kind of small piazza that is so useful in punctuating the linear network and reducing it to visually digestible sections of town.

Postscript: Loreto

An exaggeration, as every traveller knows, to pretend that internal combustion has been mastered in the Italian Peninsula—there are few more frightening things than being hunted down the street by a sportsman on a Lambretta playing his instrument for pillion-laughs. However, the Italians show more elasticity in their approach to the problem than we. To start off with they hold that the street was not made for cars alone. At Loreto the traffic stream is heavily censored. All cars and trucks except those that have business on the main street are either by-passed or parked within a few feet of the square. The censoring is done in the simplest way by a No Admittance sign favoured drivers (i.e. those who have goods to pick up or set down) are permitted to flout. A cop at the other end sees that this privilege is not abused. The street is thus about 75 per cent pedestrian as can be seen in 352. It is illustrated here because we propose

353   354

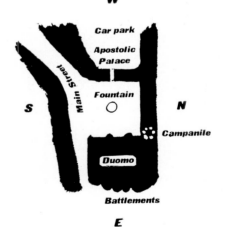

to treat Loreto as a special case (which it is) and
do it briefly in the next few pages as a test of
points already made. First, as the plan shows, the
street's entry at the S.W. *corner* of the square with
vehicular passage down one side only—the rest of
the Piazza being pedestrian. As yet all that can be
seen of it is a fraction of the Duomo and the
whole, 353, of Vanvitelli's lovely honey-coloured
Campanile of 1751, but it is enough to give an idea
of the angle at which the street enters the square
since the Campanile stands (remember S. Mark's?)
on the *corner* of the Piazza. One's guess is that
the Campanile was built on the axis of the street.

When you do get a view of the Duomo, it is worth
it. Seen through the fountain, 355, the facade
demonstrates the way good Baroque—one of its
virtues as townscape—can make the urban scene
busy without having to hire a crowd. When you

356

circle the fountain and look back, 357, the scene is still more unlikely for the west and north sides of the piazza are occupied by the Palazzo Apostolico, built (but not, of course, completed) by Bramante in 1510, now a hospice for the reception of the crippled and bedridden and their personnel who come by the 'White Train'—Loreto is a minor Lourdes—to visit the Santa Casa. The nuns in 356 are walking out through the great entrance archway towards a fine example of trapped sky in which the sun can be seen to set on March 21st and September 22nd. More than usually due west, that is, and beyond the archway is the car-park, totally invisible though only one second away. No cars are allowed through—the Piazza is pedestrian. Reduced in size, sky and arch are seen again in 357, this time in their fabulous context.

216

358

359

360
361

Difficult to put into words the full effect the Piazza
has on the mind. One can only say that after S.
Mark's it is probably the most perfect open space
in Italy and belongs to the free-floor-area
type, 359, 360, as opposed to that other Italian
speciality (mentioned already) the quart-in-pint-
pot (standard example, the Trevi Fountain).
The Piazza della Madonna has everything, great
architecture, of several periods, foiled by a
vernacular flank (that of the street), 358, and
married to a lay-out which is both deeply romantic
and extremely practical—the insulation of the
car-park is in itself an object lesson to planners.
However, the surprises are not exhausted yet,
In an earlier note (on Sabbioneta) the word
surprise was used to denote the satisfaction
one specialist eye feels at being taken for a visual
ride by another specialist eye. A mellow aesthetic
pleasure. When the word is used here it means
something different—profound astonishment. Awe
is not too strong for the sensation which bludgeons
the rubberneck, when, having exhausted the Piazza,
he continues down the main street and disappears
along the southern flank of the Duomo. Keeping
it on his left, that is, or, if he is moving backwards
like the camera, 361, right. *Disappears*, because the

362

363, 364
365

street takes a steep dive here into a rabbit hole
whose sides are suddenly crowned by a series of
battlements. They are very high and very heavily
battered and give rise, 363, 364, 365, to plastic
undulations reminiscent of Scots castles and
Yorkshire Moores. The shock is indescribable. We
cannot discuss here why the Cathedral and its
surroundings were fortified, but fortified they were
and fortified they remain and the fortifications
have to be seen to be believed. The building behind
the priest and his party, 362, who have just come
to the bottom of the rabbit hole, is, believe it or
not, the Duomo. When one remembers the facade,
surprise seems a fair word to use. And when on the
last tack one is able to get a view back, comes the
climax. The combination of these fantastic

corbelled ramparts and Guiliano Sangallo's dome,
367, shining like a crystal temple straight out of
the Celestial City, makes a kind of music not often
heard in this hard world. The sublime in
townscape, proof that the battle of the styles
doesn't have to be a shooting war. Either then or
now. The factory on the Verona road, 370, differs
from the Cathedral battlements, 369, no more
profoundly than do the battlements from
Bramante's Palazzo Apostolico, 368, and there is
no reason why, with the exercise of understanding
and sympathy, contemporary architecture
shouldn't achieve just such triumphs of contrast
as Sangallo's dome.

366

A high-flown sentiment but Loreto, hot-bed of
devotion that it is, encourages an intemperate
emotional climate. To the near-hysteria of the
townscape addict has to be added an electric
atmosphere of faith as the sick and dying are
brought in to take their chance of a miracle in
the Cathedral where beds and bathchairs queue
up to enter the Santa Casa, cottage of the Virgin
Mary and Joseph, transported here by angels from
Nazareth on the night of December 9th, 1294, and

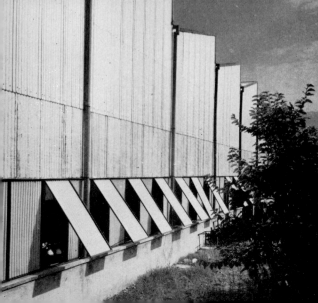

368
369
370, 371

given the treatment by Bramante, Sansovino, Sangallo the elder, Sangallo the younger, the Lombardo brothers, the Della Porta brothers and Bandinelli. The angelic porterage is depicted in the relief, 382, on Recanati Tower. Since the queue contains every known idiocy, deformity, disease, disfigurement, one might expect the emotions to be grim ones but here Loreto springs its last and greatest surprise for the keynote is gaiety. Nurses, nuns, clergy, patients—all have the air of being out on a spree. Which is exactly what they are out on. A spree from life with its laws of nature, deadly utilitarianism, rejection of magic. The saints having taken over, a sort of sanity supervenes, and sanity and gaiety are close acquaintances. On gala occasions when an altar is set up on the fountain in the Piazza and the sick laid out in battle order to be blessed by the bishop, 371, at certain climacterics in the service the street traffic is stopped. Then come moments of tremendous theatre with tough Commie truck-drivers lounging by their cabs and mentally machine-gunning the scene while tragedy stalks the beds where nuns and nurses cherish cripples, spastics, infants and all-but-corpses. The quintessence, this, of urban drama, in no way lessened by the actions of the other kind of truck-drivers who kneel right there on the tarmac. Should anyone demand an illustration of the definition of townscape on page 12 this is it.

8

Air

As explained already the divisions in this book though arbitrary
have been made with a purpose, the intention of which may at
this point become clearer. All buildings use air, but some use
more air than others. In short are more airy. Or more aerated. The
Public Authority approach to air, which is simply the public
health approach, is not the artist's. Or anyway not the architect's. The great architects (if not always the great painters)
have generally been sensitive to air itself, as *air*, or, if you prefer
it, *space*, the translucent element in which all the affairs of man
take place as surely as fish use water. And the transition from the
too, too solid bulk of 'Norman' to the airy palaces of the twentieth century is in a sense the history of architecture. Inside or
out, architecture is basically the art of arranging space and that
architecture is the fittest which makes the observer most aware
of what it is doing.

The point is made here to explain why certain Bolognese arcades, which have nothing to distinguish them from their pre-

decessors except this preoccupation with space, have been selected for this section rather than the one before. It is as though they had glass sides and were otherwise sealed in order to contain without leakage this precious element which in the event becomes almost visible, and so reveals the artist's purpose: to pass on this revelation to the man-in-space, make him conscious of what he isn't normally alive to, the envelope which forms his frame of reference. So regarded, the arcading on pages 228-9 becomes less a series of architectural motifs than a series of space-frames encouraging the observer to view his relationship to 'objects' in a new light, that of the fish in the aquarium, capable in this case however of pushing through the glass, Alice-wise, into the next goldfish bowl. And the next.

Serial space. Towers, fountains and trees carry out the function of weeds in the same operation, that of realizing the medium in which the body has its being.

372

373

Serial Space

So far arcading has been treated as one of many
street variants, as a way that is of closing or
enclosing the vista, 372, 373, but this is only one of
its functions. The arcade's second townscape virtue
lies in its ability to do just the opposite, act as a
lid without sides and thus as a natural creator of
space-bodies. Not necessarily the elementary ones
of the piazza either, for it shares with glass the
ability to define the foreground without prejudice
to background and middle distance and so provides
the opportunity for more complicated figures which
can be explored progressively as a succession of
frames, or chain of space-events. At its best the
effect is of archipelagos of space-bodies, one space-
island swimming into the picture behind the other.
Serial space. This study ends with one of the most
delightful of such, shown here, 374 and 375, in the
spirit if not quite the letter of the original, a

374

pedestrian piazza surrounded by cloisters one of
which doubles as the side-walk to the street, a
main traffic artery, with the traffic stream placed
by this means behind bars but not lost to view, so
providing the piazza with protection from dead-
area dangers. The archipelagos are all around one
here, an example of what contemporary planners
could do with different materials but the same
results at, say, Piccadilly Circus or Knightsbridge
Green. Remembering (as northerners) that the sun
is no longer the top priority now that neon has
taken over its principal function of dispersing
gloom and despondency. Remembering also that
the cloisters of Bologna, doyen of arcaded cities,
were built against the Northern rains rather than
the Southern suns.

Sharp Instrument

There are various other ways of drawing attention
to Space, always in danger as it is of being left out
of things. One is to cut it cruelly with the sharp
instruments used at Verona on the Ponte Scaligero,
376, built in 1354, damaged by flood waters of the
Adige, restored in the sixteenth century,
destroyed by the Germans in the last war and
magnificently rebuilt in 1950. Or the even sharper
ones on the Duomo, 377, at Mantua. For this
purpose a Ghibelline crenellation is more effective
than a Guelf. The medieval builders knew a lot

more than we do about piercing space and so did
the painters who used the sharp instrument
regularly as a formal theme. The Mantuan gables
are an example. They reappear accurate in every
detail in a painting of 1494, *La Cacciata dei Bonacolsi*,
in the Palazzo Ducale, interesting historically
because it represents the day of August 13th, 1328,
when the Gonzagas liquidated Passerino Bonacolsi,
captain of the city, seized Mantua and established
a dictatorship which lasted until the eighteenth
century.

377

378

379

The Big Leak

The subtlety of the Tarquinian stage-set, 347, lay in exploiting the sky as back-drop by means unconnected with what was said earlier on the subject of trapping. Nevertheless the big leak remains a threat wherever buildings are low and enclosures wide. London has always suffered from too much sky. The Italian insurance against the threat, a surprisingly successful one, consists of those soaring often disconnected towers which seem to take the fight out of heaven. They come in three sizes, starting with modest gate towers like that at Bardolino, 378. Hardly worthy of a mention one might think, until the removal of a few feet of

pasteboard, 379, reveals the important job it does. Este, 380, and Padua, 381, Verona, 384, and Mantua, 385, belong in the same league and rely on titivations and change of materials for their ability to push back the sky. Secondly, the Great Gesture, represented by the Campanile of S. Mark's, or the less famous Recanati Stump, 382. Thirdly, the frankly mad Alberti's Grove of Spires—hailing from Siena, 383, and Bologna, 386, and fundamentalist to the last brick. The two first come within the category of architecture, the third belongs to the realm of violence, insane but fascinating, to be cherished for its excess and more worth while than lorry-loads of nothing-too-much.

382

383

384

385

386

387

388

Air

So far the discussion has been carried on as though
the thing in question, Space, existed as a vacuum.
In point of fact terrestrial space is an apparently
infinite volume occupied by an invisible gas called
air, and *air* and *space* are two different articles
posing separate townscape problems, the latter
susceptible to architectural treatment, the former
not. One of the reasons, this, why trees, which
react to air as well as space, are important as

236

389

urban accessories. An earlier note on motion
deliberately ignored their function as mobiles in
the interest of the pigeon cult, but while an
airborne bird is not to be despised, trees remain
the familiar instrument of 'wind' and so the *air's* or
atmosphere's most puissant means of expression.
Space explorers too, of course. The cypress in 388
makes in its way just as dynamic a raid into space
as the fountain in 387, and either as equivalents,
389, 390, 391, or foils, 392, they offer the town
precisely the relief sponges on match sticks provide

390

391, 392

for a child's building blocks. Mobile against stabile.
Free form versus geometry. Certain soils and
temperatures favour one tree rather than another,
palms on the Riviera, 393, 396, conifers in
Scandinavia, but by and large it can be said that
Europe is populated by the same varieties.
Nationalism easily beats geography here, however,
and an avatar from another star who expected the
continent to have a uniform look would be in for a
surprise. Having used up most of their big trees
the Italians are forced to specialize in soft woods
and quick growing timber. A dilemma that is not
in any way unique, yet no other nation can match
the effects they have achieved with young planting.
Conifers are notoriously tricky to handle for
landscape purposes and in England almost always
look out of place but the Italians have a genius

393

397

for mixing species, 395, in a way that achieves
informality and variety. A difficult thing to do
with evergreens. More difficult still, the Municipal
Park-scape which achieves formality without
tedium. This one, 394, is in the worst sense

ornamental yet remains as fresh and exciting as a
Daniell print of an Indian jungle. Very studied,
but effects at least as ornamental are achieved by
totally different means in the Po valley where
poplars, 397, are planted as a crop.

399
400

All Creeping Things

Because in silviculture there is a descending scale
from forest tree, 398, through soft wood and
sapling to the small fry of the woodland world,
shrub, bush, creeper, wall plant, pot-plant, it
doesn't follow that the big stuff is a more
important element in townscape than the small.
These two views of the great wall of the Palazzo
at Capodimonte, 399, 400, show the variety
of plants (not overlooking the hair on the wall)
that can be packed into a small area without
prejudice to the architectural form. A special plea

243

might be made here for that doyen of creeping things, polygonum (the climbing variety), a plant of fantastic growth and hardihood, ready to accept the most ruthless crew-cut, as much at home in the sootiest city as the sandiest plain, always happy to climb the tallest tree and ready to produce on demand a wealth of flower as well as foliage. In the south of Europe it comes rightly second to the vine but in England polygonum might well be

244

used as a substitute (and sometimes is). It is no killer either. Here, 401, it has invaded a forest tree, providing in the process a featherbed of milky foam which makes an ideal antidote to the fortress walls and gleaming dome of a building we already know, the Duomo at Loreto. Comparison with 367 will show the kind of transformation imaginative planting can create.

9

Fire

In the South, sunlight is an enemy, in the North a friend. The corollary, that in the south Civilia requires as little sky as it can get and north as much, is false however, since rain and blight are every bit as much a menace to the citizen's morale as sun and sweat. Cut out as much of it as you decently can, is a good practical precept for the townscaper, without going so far as to banish the contrasts which make blinding rain in the street the appropriate foil to a cosy neon-lit arcade, a combination which can be seen at its best once again in Bologna, that model of urbanity. We British tend to think of our climate as a liability Italians and other fortunate races don't share; and of the wide difference in gaiety between cities north and south of, say, Lyons, as a by-blow of temperature and rainfall.

To this argument Bologna supplies the classic refutation. Go there in November, when fog and rain attack the plain of Lombardy, if you want to discover just how good a British Civilia could be were the planners to exploit rather than shrug off the climate. The neon-lit arcades, the rolling fog in the roadway outside, the

245

muted traffic, the jolly 'feel' of invisible crowds going about their pleasures in safety in grottos ablaze with mystic fire make unforgettable townscape.

Safety is the key-word here with its pay-off in effervescence; safe within their brilliant cave the citizens can afford to enjoy the contrasts nature, damp in tooth and claw, provides outside. Comparing this spritely near-interior life with the grim misery of a London fog one sees the error of accepting defeat at the hands of the national climate. Two things account for Bologna's achievement, shelter and fire, arcades and neon, of which the second (electricity) adds up to the greatest urban revolution since steam, providing as it does twenty-four hours of canned sunshine a day anywhere you like in the world. Of this the Romans have been quick to take advantage with the best flood-lighting in Europe.

As to the natural fire, in countries where sunlight is at a discount and light and shade play hard-to-get, there is and always has been an alternative, or perhaps one should say a variation—colour. One thinks again not of green glazed tiles and blood-red bricks but of the nautical tradition and the old seaport trick of obtaining shadow by architectural means, tarring the weather side of a coastguard station, or outlining in whitewash the functional parts of a drawbridge or the important apertures of a quayside warehouse.

Light

Popular superstition contrasts the grey North with
the colourful South but the true situation is—or
should be—precisely the reverse. Between them the
sun and the shadows it throws in the countries
where it shines and throws shadows, 402, 403, 404,
405, make the use of bright colours redundant or
(by bleaching) unfeasible, so that the urban South
leans towards desert tones and earth tints,
rendered dramatic and brilliant by light and
shade. It isn't the fault of Northern planners if
their sun refuses to shine with the same
brilliance. It *is* their fault if they fail to find

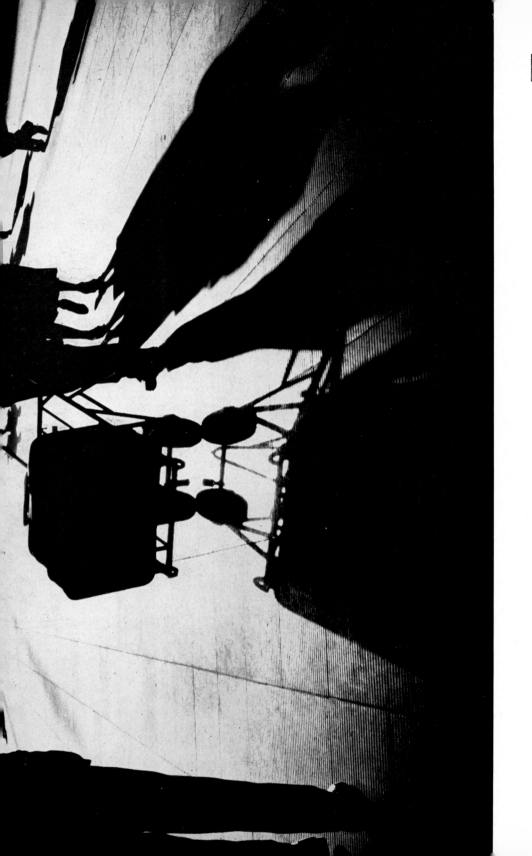

alternatives to light and shade, the most obvious
of which is colour. Used preferably as make-up—
as an application that is (paint) rather than a
built-in colour in the shape for instance of those
terrifying green tiles spec builders love to use for
roofing bungalow towns. Nash and the Regency
architects knew what they were about when they
went in for stucco, but harling, as examples at
Cumbernauld show, can produce effects just as
gay. In general, the rule is, the greyer the day the
nearer colours should get to black and white,
remembering, however, that by night North and
South stand suddenly on equal terms, and here the
Italians have established a clear superiority in the
use both of neon, 406-8, and flood lighting: which
proves that their successes are not merely due to an
accident of sunlight.

405

Fire

Floodlighting

Floodlighting in Rome is one of the best done jobs
in a city abounding in good jobs—concealed lights
throw shadows in exciting places and never a direct
light is seen. The splendid effect of S. Peter's, 409,
and S. Angelo, 419, is due to the intelligent efforts
of the Sempietrini, a guild of men founded
when the building was completed (this guild is
responsible for the general upkeep of the fabric
as well as the floodlighting; daylight decorations
too when the occasion arises). On festas, *fiaccole*
(great bowls of burning oil) are used at night, as well
as floodlights. Generally speaking the bigger the

251

410

411, 412

Fire

celebration, the more the fun, the brighter the lights. Various techniques are used by the technological office of the Municipality who are responsible for lighting the rest of Rome, other than S. Peter's and its immediate vicinity. Panoramas such as Caesar's Forum, 410, seen from the Capitol, and Trinita dei Monti, 414, are lighted by 5,000-watt incandescent lamps in parabolic mirrors and the greenery-yallery impression of the foliage by mercury vapour lamps. On Romulus's birthday the interior of the Coliseum, 412, is blood red, an effect caused by

414

coloured filters, the use of which the Romans understand so well. Marcus Aurelius, 413, silhouetted against Michelangelo's buildings on the Capitol, is one of the high spots of a drive around Rome after dark. The fountain in the forecourt of S. Peter's, 415, another effort of the Sempietrini, allows only the spouts of water thrown into the night sky to be illuminated—very effective this.

417

415

416

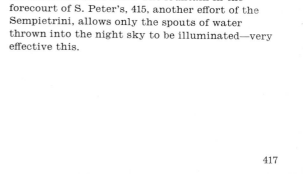

The Naiads fountain, Piazza dell' Esedra, 416, the Lion fountain, Piazza dell Popolo, 417, and that fountain of all fountains, Bernini's in the Piazza Navona, 418, are all illuminated by soft diffused lights, some above, some under water, concealing almost always all sources of light, and producing an army of moving shadows as the jets of water break the surface of the pools.

418

Reflections are used wherever possible. S. Francesca Romana, 421, is seen doubled in the pool of the Vestal Virgins as is also Castel S'Angelo, 419, seen lighted by fiaccole for the Dogma. Trajan's column, 423, and the Portico of the Temple of Antoninus and Faustina, 422, are two of the *musts* to be seen by anyone wishing to grasp the full meaning of what could be done for Civilia by intelligent lighting of its monuments.

Illustrations also show the Arches of Constantine, 411, and Septimus Severus, 420.

419

Fire

420,   423

421
422

10

Water

Consider what water has meant to Venice. In the early days of the
Republic it defended her from her enemies, later it carried her
trade; later still fresh invasions from beyond the Alps and Danube
brought the vandals back, water-worshippers by this time, cast-
ing gold into her lap for the right to billet their legions in her
gondolas. Nature deals the town-planner two perpetual wild cards,
water and a hill. Hills provide views and an opportunity for build-
up, but the hardship of climbing them sometimes quite wrongly
discourages their use.

Water's liabilities have a way of becoming its assets. It is
iridescent, goes up and down yet remains flat, charms, hypnotises,
invites you in or over by putting the obstacle of itself in the way.
An element which is genuinely elemental, it provides a foil to
modern pressures, an antidote to levity in the form of danger,
recuperative sounds, elegiac sights, aboriginal smells. The range
of its moods is wider far than those of any other natural phenomenon, hence as an expander of Civilia's emotional compass it is
in a class by itself.

Obviously, therefore, those who approach town-planning as the art of providing an acre on which to put twelve houses, and urbanism as the practice of ensuring that, like cricket, upon that acre nothing happens, will give it a wide berth.

They do. With the honourable exception of Hook New Town, which tried to play with the stuff and was promptly torpedoed and sent to the bottom, none of the New Towns of England has dared to dabble with water except in the shape of a genteel fountain or ornamental paddling pool.

Why? Why have their sponsors spurned rivers? Why have they refused to exploit the thousands of waterfront miles offered by the obsolescent canal system of the country? Why have they nowhere used a lake to create a quay or yacht basin, like Lazise? Why do so many of our existing waterfront towns in fact perform as water-*back* towns? Why in exploiting its Backs as an urban amenity should Cambridge be almost unique?

The answer lies in what passes for the official mind. From Police Commissioners to Borough Engineers water is suspect, anti-social, wet stuff, difficult to keep in order, dangerous to children. Stops circulation, threatens floods, produces fogs, favours smells. Involves bridges, attracts tin cans, dead cats, worn out car batteries, chamber-pots, bedsteads. How true. And (though man is vile and capable of outrage) how insane. Anyone with a spark of imagination or even humanity *knows* that, after a blonde, water is the most exciting thing in the visible world and both are vital to the urban scene.

And what is more they meld. As to the children, for one who falls in a hundred perhaps will escape disaster on the roads.

Water

424

Spray

To pigeons, sculpture, flags and trees, must be
added one more source of urban movement, water,
available as jets of spray in the very centre of a
city, and offering—by action, 424, a play of light and
shade—by reflection, even in puddles, 460, 461, a
world of make-believe. The puddle is in fact water's

natural archeform, the greater ones providing the
townscaper with some of his most stimulating
opportunities in the shape of ponds, lakes and
seas. A town can hardly be so called that
doesn't make play with one or more of these,
each demanding specific treatment, as the shots
that follow are designed to show.

425

H₂O

The only absolutely fool- or knave-proof way of
making a clean break between the urban thing
and its converse, the work of nature, is
water. Even British-style subtopia has not been
able to beat the sea. And being even more 'natural'
than agriculture, water provides the ultimate
contrast with town, hence the eternal drama of the
waterfront in cities fortunate enough to have one.

Water

And hence the extra excitement when artful
architects heighten the contrast by presenting to
the water—the most savage of all the elements—
a Front of the urbane, pasteboard, patched-and-
powdered gentility one associates with Regency
Brighton-and-Hove. There was a time when the
jingling open carriage together with the rest of the
traffic on the street actually heightened these
contrasts, but the road has now joined the railway
as a menace to amenity and should, as a general
principle, be banished—though not very far—from
the Promenade. All the towns on this page have
that in common, a pedestrian water-front.
Capodimonte's, 426, hardly exists even as that.
Alassio's, 427, combines the beautiful gleaming
washing at one end with civilities between
promenading rentiers at the other, English many
of them like (one suspects) the figure in 425:
typical of the funk-hole class of wasters and
drones who keep such places going through the
winter months (this shot was taken on Christmas
Eve). Giglio, 428, achieves that most moving of all
conjunctions, little painted houses and big
painted boats, Lazise, 433, 434, provides the sort
of ideal Italian dream-world we now connect with
sultry holiday passion in women's glossies.
In each of them you can live it up without the
intrusion of a traffic stream that is always trying
to substitute noise for vitality and perpetual
motion for life. Sit it out. Take what comes

430, 431,
432

433

in the way of boats, bathers, fish, foreigners,
the whole town (like Plato's) joined together into
one house—one cafe in the case of Lazise.
But the traffic doesn't want to get too far
away. The dead area is always a threat. The
traditional solution is the obvious one, to

434

interpose a building frontage between the
boulevard and the water and then add a pedestrian
promenade, 429, on the waterside. In 430 and 431—
Alassio (sea), Verona (river)—the camera is set up
in the boulevard and the pedestrians are wooing
the water. This arrangement ensures parallelism
between the vehicular and pedestrian flow, in
general a good principle because it reassures the
foot slogger that he can get back on the town
and bus—to be sequestered and then left to die
of hunger and thirst is his abiding dread.
Water isn't, of course, a necessary party to this
combination. One thinks of Bath and Brussels and
Palladio's noble service for pedestrians at Vicenza.

437
438

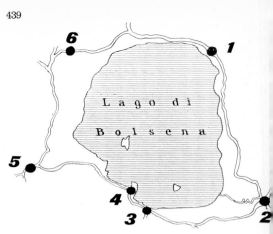

439

existing road plan

key
1, Bolsena
2, Montefiascone
3, Marta
4, Capodimonte
5, Valentano
6, Gradoli

existing road system
proposed esplanade
existing road system linked to esplanade
to create a *strada panoramica*

440

proposed esplanade

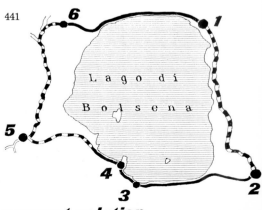

441

correct solution

top 442, 443, 444, bottom 445, 446, 447

Bridgehead Principle

Exceptions to the boulevard rule are of course common and involve the correct treatment of lakes and even ponds. To take a lake, as Garda, Como, Iseo, Maggiore have been taken and ring the entire waterfront with a motor-cum-pedestrian way at or near shore-level is to perpetuate the kind of nineteenth-century crime one hoped the twentieth century had grown out of. Yet the local authority at Viterbo decided to do exactly that, 440, to the lake of Bolsena, 435-6, perhaps the last remote big lake in Western Europe. Access must be provided to such an amenity in the interests of the public, but if in providing access you destroy the amenity your labour is in vain. The proper precedent is the bridgehead as opposed to the boulevard. Bring the cars and charas in contact with the thing at a given point but stop there and turn the vehicular traffic back or away, 441. Should closer acquaintance be required, those who want it can always get out and walk. At Bolsena the crime is already being perpetrated in all its beastliness as 442 to 447 show. The *strada panoramica*, 442, comes down from the hills at Montefiascone and becomes an Esplanade. Immediately a wire fence makes its appearance. When it reaches the lake a vast car park, 443, is created with bijou villas for company, 444, front hedge of blue conifers. Two foreign importations already—wire and blue conifers. When hedges have to be planted (as they should wherever wire is laid down) mixed deciduous is a *must*, ornamental evergreen (everblue in this case) a must *not*. 445, an unfinished stretch of the Esplanade designed to ring the entire lake, 446, 447, men at work clearing the ground at the road-head for the next section. In the end if this work is proceeded with, Bolsena, 437, 438, will join the other lakes of Europe as a Sunday afternooners' car-park, a travesty of the real purpose of recreation. A total loss, that is, as a relief from urban pressures.

From what has been said you might attribute Bolsena's current but now menaced remoteness to bush conditions and lack of tracks. In fact it is honeycombed with roads of the type shown in 448, ways cut through a jungle of bamboo, serving peasant and fisherman, hiker, too, should he be so inclined. Why not cut the bamboo, clear the ground, tar the road, add a pavement and line the whole thing with bungalows and blue conifers? Indeed, why not ? The perpetual modern dilemma : destroying the amenity on the plea of enjoying it. Bungaloid values imply a bungaloid world. The Urban ideal demands something else, a clear antithesis between town and country : the civic thing, Civilia, and its counterpart, Nature, not necessarily in the raw.

448

449, 450
451

Quays

Speaking generally the river requires a treatment
precisely the opposite to that of the lake.
Artificial banks and esplanades nearly always
enhance its charms and in the city anyway any
suggestion of a natural bank is distressing. At
Verona, Florence and Rome waterfronts which
ought to be noble are made scruffy by stones, 449,
grass, 454, and mud, 450. But there is a solution and
Rome, as we saw earlier, is taking it by building
low-level quays *below* the retaining wall of the
boulevard, an action which is entirely
revolutionizing the appearance of the Tiber, 451,
in substituting for mud a splendid geometry of
stone and concrete.

452, 453,
454

455

Flatness

The quays of Rome are solid, mud-resisting and remote, but they are also flat, as flat as your hat, and that flatness has been preserved against all temptations to accent it with signs, warnings, railings, lamps, bollards, indeed punctuations of any sort, except those that emphasize its flatness.

The white kerb, for instance, 455, which executes a tremendous wheel in step with the river bend. More fundamentalism here. Such noble simplicity in a city inevitably overcrowded with incident furnishes what is badly needed, visual relief, a wide belt of it, encircling the whole town and offering the subtle kind of amenity one expects of Civilia. By comparison, the next reach, 454, where the quay has yet to be built, is a shambles.

456
457

458

459

Immediacy

As a postscript to water it might be worth
underlining the obvious by emphasizing the
difference in sheer weight of armour between
lakeside and seaside constructions even when the
lake is as big as Maggiore and the sea as cosy as
the Mediterranean. The ocean, 458, always calls
for massive defences while one of the charms of the
lakeside lido, 456, 457, 459, is the sense of immediacy
that arises from the closer contact between water
and user, 452, 453, made possible by the
domestication of the one and the increase in
self-confidence of the other.

460

461

11

Conclusions

Townscape deals with foils, focal points, fluctuation, vistas closed and vistas open, truncation, change of level, perspective, silhouette, intricacy, anticipation, continuity, space, enclosure, exposure, the precinct, profile. These and a hundred other issues debated over the post-war years in *The Architectural Review* have now been collected into one of the seminal books of the century, *Townscape* by Gordon Cullen.*

A big book. Anyone whose emotions are involved in a home-town or adopted city is advised to build a poacher's pocket inside his jacket to carry this big book around until he knows each of its many morals by heart. The present study will be doing all that can be expected in isolating one moral, the one which defines the city as the product of the gregarious law, the law, that is, of gravitation, under which bodies of people are drawn (forget Einstein, remember Poe) to their own centre of gravity. An action which, as with gravitation, generates heat, in this case (Gordon Cullen) *civic warmth*, the climate whose lucent airs cause the urban organism to burgeon so that its sons and daughters wax great and multiply. Multiplication of sons and daughters involves multiple use, multiple use involves a pattern designed to provide the maximum number of services, amenities, entertainments per foot super. The consequence, congestion. Not, please note, the congestion of a flaccid, congealed lump of cold suet (ours today); a complex order, rather, arising from the elaborate productive, interlacing of trades, crafts, paths and people—in figures of such complexity as to remind one of the motions of a planetarium, on the surface wholly arbitrary and whimsical, but at a deeper level the product of subtle harmonies.

That is the key-note—harmony, within diversity. Vividly evoked by

---

* *Townscape* by Gordon Cullen. London: The Architectural Press.

H. B. Creswell's description of the Strand in the 90s,* hedged by a maze of continuous alleys and courts and 'fronted by numbers of little restaurants whose windows vaunted exquisite feeding; taverns, dives, oyster and wine bars, ham and beef shops; and small shops marketing a lively variety of curious or workaday things all standing in rank, shoulder to shoulder, to fill the spaces between its many theatres.' As shop elbows shop and shoulder squeezes shoulder, one watches the gaps between the buildings inexorably filling up, until with the latest oyster bar making its dive between the small shop and the large theatre—presto—*the street*.

For in the end that is what congestion, dynamic and gravitating, comes down to. The street. *Multiple use invokes the street.* If (to be honest for once) one concedes the Prairies, Airies and Fairies their moments, nothing they can pull out of the bag will ever prejudice for long the first axiom of town-planning. Which is, that the unit of the city is the street.

There was a time when this statement would have sounded dangerously like a cliché. Today, so far have we gone (quite rightly) down the path of pedestrianism, precinctualism, segregation, decentralization—so far has the *city street*, crowded, vital, lived on and variously used, faded out of the planner's schedule of requirements—that the idea sounds almost revolutionary even when the word means anything or nothing—maze of alleys off the Strand, laburnums and mowing machines back there in Arcadia, residential-urban, shopping-arterial, commercial-industrial, or just the pallid, bloodless negation which passes itself off as street in the dull eye of the devitalized townee. One thinks in this context of the Japanese who refuse to name streets because they are nothing but the spaces between buildings.

That attitude would have shocked the great man who has figured throughout this study as the first modern townscaper, the first man in history, perhaps, to establish a street hierarchy, Alberti. Highways, his list started with, headed by one that gave him a lot of pleasure, the dual carriageway already existing between Ostia and Rome. After highways came high streets, then just streets, then ways, lanes, intricate ways, 'turn-again streets without any passage through' (the U-trap), and 'smaller, short streets running across from one great street to another; not to be as a direct public way, but only as a passage to some house that fronts it' (the T-trap). The irony is that half a millennium later we haven't got any further. Some would say we hadn't got as far.

And this is not the place to start. However, a single point might be

---

* *The Architectural Review*, December 1958.

worth making, which is that despite their diversity there is one thing both the maze of alleys and the laburnums have or ought to have in common: intimacy, the pedestrian, the human scale. The early fathers of the garden city movement set out to provide exactly this cosy human scale and did sometimes succeed in creating little enclaves which they called Closes. Howard's Close (not End). Which is exactly what the street one lives a life in should aim to be—not an Open, a Close. When it is close enough the traffic problem has to move elsewhere, thus removing the cry for Radburns unlimited—to run down a child at 10 mph isn't at all easy. There would be another notch for the belt if we could convince, first ourselves, then our public servants, that the street, customary and canon, is not, first, a traffic artery but a stage-set, built for drama in many acts; and for a large cast with parts less tedious than Shakespeare's irksome Temperance Seven. That goes for the alleys off the Strand as much as for Arcadia and its laburnums. More so. Even more than Arcadia the alleys are *occupied territory* (Cullen again), the headquarters of an army-of-occupation whose *persona* remains constant through every shift of personnel, exercising, one hopes, the benevolent authority proper to an occupier and enjoyer by making the most of the available perquisites—sitting in the sun, smoking in the rain, day-dreaming, pottering, loitering (Notice in a Scots town: NO LOITERING ON THIS CORNER. BY ORDER), window-shopping, reading, watching, leaning, chatting, drinking. Also having children and giving them an embrasure of pavement for play. These are not privileges but the basic services the street must provide before it even begins to think of itself as a thoroughfare. Periodic occupations they can be called and must be woven, as Gordon Cullen suggests, into the fabric itself in the shape of floor patterns and punctuations, recessions in the building line, enclosures, deflections, changes of level. And, once woven in, taken over by the army of occupation, and defended in depth, with one up the spout for those absentee landlords, the Borough engineer and the Borough surveyor, who lurk there in the wings awaiting the opportunity to iron the whole thing out in the cause of smooth, fast, relentless traffic-flow.*

Closeness instead of openness. End of the Bye-law traffic artery. The occupation of the street by those who are *on* it at the expense of its throughness. This the Italians always well understood and matched their understanding with their acts, though in recent years the scooter has undone some of the good work. The theme-song of this philosophy, it's a long lane that has no turning, was incorporated into the folk-lore of the

---

* If there's one thing they hate it's a maze of alleys. They soon got rid of the Strand's.

race a long time ago, but we are an unconscionable time a-learning.

Why? Because we have no humility. We think we are good and we aren't good. A bird's-eye view of town-planning in this century reveals the richness of our resources and the poverty of imagination that has the disposing of them. There is something frightening about a world that combines honest worth, technical know-how, good intentions, a bottomless bank-balance and an utter bankruptcy of ideas. Visual ones we speak of here but their absence is a symptom of other vital bankruptcies, emotional and intellectual, which have led the New World (for example), once the redresser of the Old, to redress herself in terms of the mining camp and used-car lot. The gap between potential and performance in this generation is far more sinister than any bomb or budgetary deficiency.

Nor is the disease, chronic as it is, susceptible to any single cure. Nevertheless, amongst the roads back to health one at least is paved not with intentions but performances, the good performances of people who knew what they were up to and acted accordingly. First and foremost, as we have seen, the Italians, who may even yet find a formula to reconcile progress with order. Lest they fail the pressing need now is to make an appreciation of the surviving tradition of townscape before its streets are torn up and paved, bumper to bumper, with the coach-work of Global Tours.

280